PETER
FISHERMAN, DISCIPLE, APOSTLE

Happy Anniversary
My love.

田

Me.

PETER

FISHERMAN
DISCIPLE
APOSTLE

F. B. Meyer

CHRISTIAN LITERATURE CRUSADE
Fort Washington, Pennsylvania 19034

CHRISTIAN LITERATURE CRUSADE
Fort Washington, Pennsylvania 19034

CANADA
1757 Avenue Road, Toronto, Ontario M5M 3Y8

Originally published by
Fleming H. Revell Co.

Published in the United Kingdom by
Marshall, Morgan & Scott Ltd.

This American edition 1978
under special arrangement with
the British publisher.

SBN 87508-349-8

FOREWORD

PETER COMES nearer to us than any of his brother Apostles. We revere James, the brother of our Lord, for his austere saintliness. We strain our eyes in the effort to follow John to the serene heights, whither his eagle-wing bore him. But Peter is so human, so like ourselves in his downsittings and uprisings, so compassed with infirmity, that we are encouraged to hope that perhaps the Great Potter may be able to make something even of our common clay.

When walking over his farmstead with a friend we came on a field, which on a former visit appeared to be choked with thistles. He had bought it at a cheap rate because of its derelict condition. But it had been carefully drained and enriched. Much care and science had been expended on it, and to my friend's surprise a rich crop of clover resulted. The long-buried seed had lain starved and hopeless in the soil till the rich culture had called it into evidence.

It needed the Saviour's insight to discover an Apostle in Simon Bar-jona, the fisherman; and the Saviour's patient culture to elicit the dormant qualities of his character, which speak in every paragraph of his Epistles, and fitted him to be the leader of the Primitive Church. But if the Master could do so much for him, what may He not effect, my reader, for thee and me?

F. B. MEYER.

CONTENTS

I

INTRODUCTORY

MATT. iii. 1–12; MARK i. 1–8; JOHN i. 35–42.

"Where is the lore the Baptist taught,
The soul unswerving and the fearless tongue?
The much enduring wisdom, sought
By lonely prayer the haunted rocks among?
Who counts it gain
His light should wane
So the whole world to Jesus throng?"

Keble.

THE CONTRAST between the method of the Divine Worker and the human is specially apparent in the earliest stages. *Man,* with considerable confidence in his own powers of initiation and fulfilment, cries: "Go to, let *us* build a tower the top of which shall reach to heaven, so that we be not scattered abroad." *God* begins in secret, and works curiously in the lowest parts of the earth. He calls an individual from the crowd, trains him long and patiently, and finally makes him His partner, the centre of a new unit, the channel through which He pours Himself forth upon the world. Man's method, more often than not, ends in a Babel of confusion; whilst God's, invariably, is consummated in the city of the Living God, the Jerusalem which descends from above.

The majority of those who, from time to time, have been called to this holy service, have been selected from among the foolish, weak, and despised ranks of the human family, that the excellency of the power might be of God, and not of man. There have been thousands of noble exceptions; but, as a rule, not many wise, or great, or noble according to this world's estimate, have been called. The hole of the pit that has yielded God His materials has been of common clay, and the rock whence His stones have been hewn of very ordinary grain.

9

It is not surprising, therefore, to learn that the leader of the apostolic band was drawn from the ranks of very ordinary people, and that the story of his life opens in the obscure village of Bethsaida, at the north-west corner of the Lake of Galilee. The unadorned and simple homes of its fishermen were in striking contrast to the marble palaces of the neighbouring proud city of Capernaum, which were erected by the large incursion of Roman residents, who were attracted to the locality by its equable climate and luxuriant natural beauty. The shore was lined with costly palaces and imposing public offices; the roads were filled with splendid equipages; and luxurious gondolas flashed to and fro upon the lake.

I. THE COMING OF THE SON OF ZACHARIAS.—The native population probably held aloof from the manners and habits of the conquerors, though quite ready to take advantage of their wealthy patronage and custom. Under their breath they spoke together of the great days of Judas Maccabæus and of Judas of Galilee, before whom even the mighty Roman legions had on more than one occasion been compelled to give way. To these echoes of the memorable past were added a strange anticipation and hope, which stirred in the breast of many, that the hour was near when the invader would be driven beyond the waters of the Great Sea, and the kingdom would be once more restored to Israel. Some said that the weeks of Daniel's vision had nearly expired. Some told that the aged Simeon before his death bore witness to having held the Lord's Messiah in his arms. Some spoke of visions of angel-choirs, and said that portents and voices had been steadfastly borne witness to by creditable witnesses. "The people were in expectation and all men mused in their hearts."

All suddenly the land was startled and shaken with the rumour that God had visited His people. A company of pilgrims, crossing the Jordan by the fords of Jericho, had been arrested by a strange figure, gaunt and sinewy, the child of desert solitudes, who had accosted them with the cry: "Repent, for the Kingdom of Heaven is at hand." When released from the spell and able to proceed to Jerusalem, they could talk of nothing else. That strange figure, half Bedawin and half prophetic! That voice which rang with trumpet-note! That evident vision of the Unseen and Eternal, which illumined his face with unearthly glory! That he had no lodging but a cave! That his food consisted of locusts dipped in water and baked on the hot coals, with wild honey to make them palatable! Without wife or child! These things gripped the national imagination and thrilled the air, already charged with electricity. "The people that sat in darkness saw a great light," and on those that sat in the shadow of death, dawn arose.

The tidings spread everywhere, as by a mysterious telepathy. They reached the mountain-villages of the Lebanon to the north and the sheepfolds of Bethlehem and Hebron to the south. They were discussed by priests in the intervals between the Temple-services, and by Rulers in their council-chambers; by businessmen, as they transacted in the markets, and by traders, as they sat behind their stalls in the bazaars. Holy women, waiting at the wells for the drawing of water, spake often one to another, whilst the Lord hearkened and heard and wrote thereof in His Book of Remembrance. The little children were told to reverence the name of John, the son of Zacharias, whose parents had passed through such strange experiences at his birth.

Then the whole country rose *en masse*. It was the Sabbatic year, when the ploughmen and the vinedressers ceased from toil. Men had plenty of leisure to leave their homes and fields, their vineyards and orchards. Through a land carpeted with flowers and exhaling fragrance, the confluent streams of people poured down the Jordan Valley in eager crowds. "There went out to him Jerusalem and all Judæa, and all the region round about Jordan." Multitudes were baptized in the Jordan—confessing their sins; among whom we may surely include the brothers Andrew and Peter, and their life-long companions, James and John.

II. THE BAPTIST'S INFLUENCE ON PETER.—Peter was married, but marriage among the Orientals takes place early. He was, therefore, still in the prime of his manhood. Strong, vehement, impulsive and self-assertive, he could by no means be accounted a saint. Would he so easily have taken to swearing, when the maid accosted him in the hall of Caiaphas, unless he had been addicted to the habit in early life? He was doubtless attentive to the duties and formalities of his religion, attended the Temple-feasts, paid his dues, and was morally respectable. He was satisfied that he was a not unworthy son of

Abraham. We are reminded of those words with which Paul described his earlier life as a son of the synagogue—"I was alive without the law once."

From his youth he was an ardent patriot. Like all his friends and companions, he was prepared to sacrifice everything he possessed to see David's race once more on David's throne. When, therefore, he and the others heard the tidings of the Baptist's appearance, they hailed them as heralding the new era. Might not this be the first phase of the kingdom which the God of Heaven was setting up, and which would never be destroyed, and whose sovereignty would not be left to another people, but it would break all other kingdoms in pieces, and stand for ever?

His friends shared these convictions and hopes. Taking with them a frail canvas tent to serve as a shelter, and a bag of coins for the supply of their simple needs, Peter, his brother, and their friends bade good-bye to home and craft and "went forth to see." They crossed the Jordan by the fords of Bethabara and joined the crowds who were streaming down the Jordan Valley to the scene of the Baptist's ministry.

It must have seemed the prelude to the Day of Judgment when the Baptist, selecting a ledge of rock for his pulpit, stood forth to address the awestruck throng, gathered from all the land to listen. Clearly enough, as our Lord suggested, he was no reed shaken by the wind of popular favour. He was neither courtier nor sycophant. He spoke what he knew and testified what he had seen. There had never arisen a greater than John amid all the myriads of the human family. He penetrated the hollow pretensions of Pharisee and Scribe; compared them to the rock-vipers; threatened them with the woodsman's axe, the smelter's furnace, and the harvester's fan. In his stern outlook there was short shrift for the sinner that refused to repent. He had faith that God would yet transform the stones of the desert into sons of Abraham. Truly he was a light that burned as well as shone!

Beneath such preaching, Peter must have been deeply moved. It raked his soul. Beneath those words sin revived and he died. He felt then, as he confessed afterwards, that he was "a sinful man." Frequently, as in after years, he would go out alone and weep bitterly, and when on the Day of Pentecost he saw that vast crowd

of Jews pricked to the heart and crying out "What must we do?" he
knew exactly the agony of their remorse. Probably he was baptized
by the Baptist, confessing his sins. He had thus been born of water,
as afterwards he was to be born of the Holy Spirit.

III. PETER'S FIRST INTERVIEW WITH THE LORD.—When Jesus was
baptized he may have been present, but as yet his senses were not
annointed to behold the open heaven or discern the descending dove.
Or he may have been paying a brief visit to attend to necessary affairs
of home and business. Certainly he was out of the way, when, on
two successive days, the Baptist designated the Saviour as the Lamb
of God. But he was back again in the Jordan Valley on the morning
following the day of his brother's memorable interview with the
One whose shoe-latchet the Baptist confessed himself unworthy to
unloose.

Andrew and John had spent some hours in His holy company.
They had been welcomed to His dwelling, had listened with rapt
attention while He spake of heavenly things, had perhaps listened to
His recital of the salient features of the Temptation from which He
had just emerged, and had been told of His chosen method for
winning back the kingdom by patient sufferings rather than armed
force. As they listened their hearts had burned within them. They
knew, with absolute conviction, that they had found the Messiah;
and rejoiced with a joy exceeding all their experience.

Leaving Christ's presence, they said each to the other "We must
tell Simon of all this, so soon as we can find him"; and, as was
befitting, Andrew found him first and brought him to Jesus, saying,
"We have found the Messiah." *Brought him*, as though it was
necessary to overcome some hesitation. The young colt is difficult
to catch, as if it realizes all that the first lassoing may involve.

Peter was immensely impressed by that interview. This Teacher
was so complete a contrast to his earlier master John. Perhaps the
hardy fisherman may have been less attracted to Him than to the
sinewy son of the desert. He may not have been immediately sus-
ceptible to the grace and truth, and gentleness and purity, the
humility and selflessness of the Lamb of God. But if this was his first
impression, it was instantly succeeded by one of awe and wonder, as
those searching eyes looked into the depths of his nature, and Jesus

said, "Thou shalt be called Cephas" (the Aramean equivalent for the Greek *Peter*).

This is our Lord's method of making saints. He speaks of things that are not as though they were. When the heart is broken and contrite, as was the case with Peter, He speaks words of encouragement and cheer. He imputes righteousness where there is but the smallest germ of faith. He addresses us, not as though we had attained or were already perfect, but as following on. He awakens our expectancy by indicating possibilities of which we never supposed ourselves to be capable. Over the grave of our hope, He speaks words of Resurrection and Life.

"Ah," said Peter to himself, at the close of that interview, "He little realizes how fickle and wayward I am; now hot with impulse, then cold as the snows of Lebanon. And yet if He thought me capable of becoming rock, and evidently He does think so, why should I not, with His help, resolve to attain and apprehend that for which I have been apprehended?"

Thus our Saviour deals with us still. He tells us what we can become by the proper development of our temperament and the exercise of Divine grace; and as He speaks He imparts all needed help. We become possessed with the Divine ideal, and laid hold of by Divine strength; and thus the weakest become as David and David as the Angel of the Lord, the reed becomes a pillar in the Temple, the stone becomes a rock, and the chief of sinners the mightiest of saints.

It is said that Michael Angelo saw in the blocks of marble, which others had refused, the forms which his genius would call into being; so in very unlikely souls our Lord descries qualities of unusual strength and beauty, which He sets Himself to elicit; and His first act often is to reveal the fair hidden image and to impute it. He saw Peter in Simon, Israel in Jacob, Paul in Saul—and told them so!

II

EARLY DAYS IN THE MASTER'S COLLEGE

JOHN i. 43, iii. 30; MATT. iv. 23–25.

" What Thou hast given to me, Lord, here I bring Thee,
Odour and light, and the magic of gold,
Feet which must follow Thee, lips which must sing Thee,
Limbs which must ache for Thee ere they grow old."
C. Kingsley.

THE WONDER of that first interview with the Lord must have almost dazed the mind of Simon, the son of John. The Baptist's ministry had already stirred his soul to the depths, but this fresh and gracious Personality, so full of grace and truth, had revealed possibilities for his manhood which had never occurred to him. It seemed incredible that he should ever become known as the Rock-man. If angel voices had called to him from out of heaven, or the bushes had begun to burn with fire, he could hardly have been more astonished. That *he* could become a Man of Rock!

Yet a childless Abram had become Abraham, the father of a countless multitude; and Jacob, the subtle supplanter, had become Israel the prince; and Gideon, the least in his father's house, had delivered Israel from the Midianites. But the incongruity of his nature with that name seemed an unbridged chasm. When a similar promise was made to his great ancestor, he fell on his face and laughed; but notwithstanding, a child's laughter was heard in his tent and a child's hand was thrust into his aged grasp. Nothing was impossible with God. Already Peter's heart had opened to Christ's knock, never to close to Him again. His soul had turned to Him with passionate devotion. Let those who remember how it was with them when they first met Christ bear witness if there is aught of exaggeration in this statement. They who have once really seen His face can never rest content till they have apprehended that for which He has apprehended them.

15

WALKS AND TALKS.—Whatever may have been the fisherman's reverie, he was soon made aware that Jesus was minded to ɤo forth into Galilee, and he resolved to accompany Him. The distance to Cana from Bethabara was some thirty miles, and the little group would start on their way in the beauty of early morning. Apparently they had hardly left the scene of the Baptist's ministry, when they encountered Philip, and the fact that it is expressly recorded that he was a native of Bethsaida, "the city of Andrew and Peter," suggests that the two brethren had something to do with the Master's discovery of him and his immediate response.

This first journey in such company was the beginning of many similar experiences, until that further day when He would lead them out as far as Bethany and be parted from their sight. But it left an ineffaceable impression; for as these newly-found disciples walked with Him, and heard Him open the Scriptures, their hearts burned within them, and emotions were aroused too tumultuous for words.

When they came within sight of the little village of Cana, the white houses of which, embowered with verdure, beckoned to them as they climbed the slope from the rich Esdraelon plain, Philip seems to have hastened forward to announce his discovery to a devout friend of his—Nathanael. Apparently he found him pondering the story of the ladder that Jacob saw, when he slept and dreamed. The guileless Israelite little thought that the ladder was to be literally reared again on his lawn, that the angel-ministry was actually in operation, and that he might begin to climb the scale of ascent which would presently land him in the Divine Presence-Chamber.

Probably our Lord and His disciples remained as guests in his home, and Peter was introduced to a new friend destined to be knit with him in a life-long companionship. But it was at the marriage-feast to which they were all invited on the following day that he drank in the deepest lessons of the Master to Whom he had given his allegiance.

At first he must have been greatly startled. Until he had come under the influence of the Baptist, his highest ideal of religion had been the Curator of the Synagogue, the Pharisee with his phylacteries, and the Priests who officiated in the Temple; but their inconsistencies had only enhanced the commanding splendour of the holiness of John. Even Herod had been compelled to confess that he was "a just man and an holy." Peter and the rest were impressed and enamoured with a type of holiness that seemed so taken up with God as to be independent of the ordinary accessories of human life. John's rigid asceticism, that he seemed to have no need of a woman's love or a little child's caress, that he was absorbed in face-to-face fellowship with God, that he was absolutely fearless and unyielding—these qualities enthralled their loyalty and respect. "Ah," they remarked to each other, at the close of one of his most terrific utterances, "he speaks like Elijah or Malachi might have done; but, after all, the man is even greater than his words." When, therefore, John introduced them to Jesus, as being incomparably greater than himself, they expected the same type of holiness, in its awful, lonely splendour.

THE MARRIAGE FEAST OF CANA.—But Jesus led them to a village festival, where a group of simple peasants, principally drawn from the vineyards that terraced the adjoining hills, were celebrating a wedding. He sat there among young and old, the life of the party; His face beaming with joy, His words adding to the pleasure of the company, His presence welcomed by the children and greeted by the young lads and girls. This was an altogether new and unexpected type of holiness. Peter and the rest watched it closely, as they reclined with Jesus at the feast. What would the Baptist have done? Would he approve? Certainly this was not the religion of the Synagogue or the Temple! But as they came more and more under the spell of their wonderful Friend and Teacher, they became more profoundly convinced that this was the religion that the world was waiting for. They could not all imitate the asceticism of the Baptist in the weird loneliness of the desert. Peter, at least, was already married. But they could all follow in the steps of their new Master in the sweet amenities of the home.

And Peter learnt many things beside. That though the Lord addressed His mother with perfect respect, He was under direction from a higher source. That only a hint of need was necessary—*He* would know exactly how to meet it. That those who were called to co-operate with Him must always give Him brimfull obedience. That what His servants drew as water would blush beneath His word into the wine of the Sacrament. That He would always lead from good to better, from better to better still. These were wonderful discoveries:

and it was a happy group that left Cana when the feast was over. Jesus, and His mother, and His brethren, and His disciples went down to Capernaum. Apparently they settled that their home should be there; but as the Jews' Passover was at hand, they could not then remain many days. What a story the brothers had to tell to their father, and Peter to his wife and her mother! Bethsaida also listened, discussed the strange novelty of their transformation, and wondered greatly.

GROWING INFLUENCE OF THE MASTER.—Though probably the Master and His disciples travelled with their own families to the Feast, they met again in the precincts of the Holy City. Peter and the rest beheld with wonder their gentle and lowly Master cleanse the Temple courts as though girded with the power of an Elijah. They witnessed the signs that convinced men like Nicodemus that God was with Him. They watched the rising wrath of the Jewish magnates as they challenged the Nazarene's authority over the holy places. They pondered His affirmation that He would build the Temple in three days, though not until He was risen from the dead did they understand that cryptic utterance. Since Peter, in his subsequent address in the house of Cornelius, expressly states that God preached peace by Jesus Christ throughout all Judæa, we may fairly infer that he at least accompanied the Master in that first great itinerary, through the very regions where Æneas, Tabitha, and Simon the Tanner, in after years, greeted him again. Probably, also, in that journey Peter and his friends had their last interview with their earliest teacher, who reminded them that he had never expected to be other than the Bridegroom's friend. "Do not grieve for me," he said in effect, as they visited him and remarked the diminished numbers that came for his baptism: "I am more than content. My joy is fulfilled. I am of the earth, earthly, and I speak of the earth; *He* has come from heaven and is above all."

Nine months were spent thus. Perhaps Peter paid occasional brief visits home; but he returned to assist the Master in the baptism of those who confessed and forsook their sins; "for Jesus Himself baptized not, but His disciples." Then, to avoid the increasing suspicion of the Pharisees, the Lord and His disciples returned through Sychar and Samaria to Cana, where apparently the party broke up. *He* returned to Nazareth, whilst *they* made for their several homes. This was probably necessitated by the gathering storm, that broke first on the head of the Baptist, whom Herod cast into the dark dungeons of the grim Castle of Machærus across the Jordan.

For a further period of nine months our Lord seems to have been unattended. He probably was in constant touch with His disciples and friends, but they were not openly associated with Him. He was quietly preparing them for the great future which awaited them, but was as yet veiled from their view. Finally, when the fate of the Baptist was sealed, and no advantage could be gained by further delay, the Master went forth alone, throughout all Galilee, "teaching in their synagogues, and preaching the Gospel of the Kingdom, and healing all manner of sickness and all manner of disease among the people; and His fame went throughout all Syria, and there followed Him great multitudes of people from Galilee, and from Decapolis, and from Jerusalem, and from Judæa, and from beyond Jordan."

Peter was aware of this mighty movement, and found it irksome to stay with his boats and nets. He dreamt of Christ by night, and watched for His coming by day. Presently the morning broke, and the Master came along the shore. That day changed the entire current of his career, and the seed sown patiently through months of quiet intercourse began to yield fruit, first the blade. . . . So take *us* unto Thy college and teach *us*, gracious Lord, we humbly beseech Thee.

III

THE SETTLEMENT AS TO THE SUPREME CONTROL

MARK i. 14–20; LUKE v. 1–11.

"The livelong night we've toiled in vain,
But at Thy gracious word,
I will let down the net again:—
Do Thou Thy will, O Lord."

Keble.

NINE BUSY months had passed. Single-handed, our Lord had been conducting His mission throughout Galilee, with an ever-increasing popularity. His speed was quickened by the tidings that the Baptist had been "delivered up." Time after time, as He returned to His home at Capernaum, where His friends and disciples seem now to have settled, He devoted Himself to their further instruction in the great principles on which His life was based, and to their preparation for the decisive moment when He should bid them leave all, rise up, and follow Him. That decisive moment came thus:

THE SCENE.—It was the early morning of an autumn day. The grey waters of the lake were beginning to laugh back to the sun, slowly rising from behind the eastern hills. The deep azure of the sky, the exquisite foliage of the oleanders, the autumn-tints on the trees and shrubs that came down almost to the water's brink, the changing lights on the hills, the white glistening snows of the mighty Hermon, which, though far distant, seemed to dominate the landscape to the north, the sob of the brimming water, combined to make a worthy setting for the supreme event in the lives of the four fishermen who were destined to influence all after-history.

They had been friends from boyhood. They were partners in their fisher's craft. They were ardent disciples and friends of Him who was moving the whole country. His life, deeds, and words were always on their lips, as they floated together over the fishing-grounds, while the stars kept vigil overhead. Probably they had been speaking of Him, as they drew to shore, after a night of fruitless toil. "Would they be seeing Him soon?"

They had disembarked, were rinsing out their seine-nets, and spreading them on the shore to dry, when they became aware of the approach of a vast crowd, which were thronging and pressing upon the person of their beloved Teacher and Friend. In a moment they had forgotten their weariness and disappointment, their hunger, and the call of their homes, and were on the alert to welcome Him. He made straight for Peter's boat and asked that it might be moored within one of the rock-lined inlets that indented the shore. There He sat and spoke to His congregation, many seated on the blocks of basalt, others standing, but all rapt and wondering at the gracious words that proceeded from His lips.

It may have been Peter's lot to steady the boat by oar or boat-hook, or if it were securely fastened, to sit in the bottom of the boat, his eyes fastened on the Master's face, drinking in each word. Never man spake like this man. He taught as one that had authority, and not as the scribes. To Peter and the rest, as they afterwards confessed, these were the words of Eternal life; and deep chords in their hearts must have vibrated, when in after days they heard in the Master's memorable High Priestly prayer: "The words which Thou hast given to me, I have given them, and they have received them, and have known of a truth that I came forth from Thee."

THE INEXORABLE COMMAND.—When our Lord is about to fashion a vessel unto honour, meet for His use, whether it be of gold and silver, or of wood and earth, He has to establish His absolute authority and right to command. There can be no parleying or argument, no hesitancy or holding back. Spirit, soul, and body must be absolutely submitted to Him, at whatever cost. The disciple must leave all and follow Him. Just as He was prepared to suffer obediently even into death, so He requires of those whom He takes into the sacred circle of inward companionship that they should arm themselves with the same mind, so that they should no longer live the rest of their time to the will of the flesh, but to the will of God.

Probably Peter and the others knew this *generally*. They could hardly have been with Him so long without realizing the force of the significant words uttered by Mary to the servants at Cana: "Whatsoever He saith unto you, do it." They were prepared to give Him their loyal allegiance in the realms of morals and duty but it was altogether startling and unexpected when, invading their own sphere, He assumed their own prerogative, and said to Peter: "Put out into the deep, and let down your nets for a draught." For a moment we may dare to assume that Peter's obedience faltered; and he expressed his hesitation in the reply: "Master, we have toiled all the night, and taken nothing."

Peter had fished these waters from boyhood. There was nothing in the craft with which he was not familiar. The habits of the fish; the hours and spots most suitable for taking them; the effect of climatic conditions: in all he was proficient. He would have hotly resented any interference on the part of other fishermen of his acquaintance; and now, he found himself suddenly confronted with a bidding which was contradicted by his experience, by the universal maxims and practice of generations, and by the bitter failure of the preceding night, which had left him jaded, weary, and out of heart.

He would be prepared to obey the slightest precept that came from the Master's lips; but how could one who had spent his days in the carpenter's workshop of a mountain village be competent to take command of a boat and direct the casting of a net! Was he to renounce himself in this also? The morning was no time for fishing; the glare of light revealed the meshes of the nets, and the fish were to be found, not in the deep, but the shallower part of the lake. The whole of the fisherfolk that might see his boat putting out at such an hour, laden with nets, and evidently prepared for fishing, would laugh and count him crazy. Is it not thus with all who have been greatly used by Christ? There is no escaping the test. At a certain moment in our experience, often long after we have become disciples, the Master comes on board the ship of our life and assumes supreme control. For a moment or an hour there may be question and hesitation. We have been wont to make our own plans, follow our own chart, take our own course, and be masters in our own craft; shall we—may we, dare we—hand over the entire command to

Christ? To what point may He not steer us! On what venture may He not engage us! At what inhospitable part of the shore may He not land us! Happy are we if, after such a moment of hesitation we reply: "Nevertheless, at Thy command I will put out even to the deep, and let down the nets for a draught." This at least is certain beyond doubt, that you can never reckon on Christ's co-partnership and blessing unless you are prepared to sail under His orders, and, like the angels, fulfil His commandments, hearkening unto the voice of His word.

It has been thus all down the ages. While the ears of the majority have been filled with the hubbub of the street and the babble of the crowd; while the children of this world have been playing in the market-places and crying to their fellows; while even the seekers after truth have been overawed by the earthquake or the strong and mighty wind, rending the mountains, the quick ear of the disciple has detected the thrilling undertones of the still small voice, as Elijah once in Horeb's cave.

Sometimes others can interpret that voice better than we. "Eli perceived that the Lord had called the child."

Sometimes it pierces to the dividing asunder of soul and spirit, of the joints and marrow; as when God bade the patriarch to offer the son of his love on Mount Moriah.

Sometimes it demands of us, as of the young man, that we should sell all that we have, and come and follow to the Cross.

But whenever it speaks, it may be detected by its constant reiteration of one note, like the sounding of a bell by the tide far out from shore. It is never "Yea and nay," but always "Yea." It often speaks in the teeth of ordinary experience and convention, and asks us to leave the beach, which we have been hugging too long. It generally offers the acid test to our faith and exposes us to the ridicule of our associates. But it is endorsed in the depths of our soul by an answering assent. It is corroborated by circumstances. God's providence bears witness to the inner voice. To disobey is to become a castaway. To yield obedience is to enter on a vast and lasting inheritance.

Christ must be Master. Rabbi must give place to LORD. His will must rule, though it seems to contradict the dearest traditions of the soul. There cannot be two captains in the boat, if it is to make a successful voyage and return at last laden to the water's edge with fish. To-day and now, let that question be decided! He has a place and a use for you, but you must surrender yourself to His disposal. Refuse to be bound by customs, circumstances, or the conventions of the shore. Make Christ Captain, whilst you take to the oars! At His bidding, launch out into the deep, and remember that yonder, across the waters, is the coast-line of Eternity, where in the morning-dawn the Fire and Provision of Divine Preparation await the obedient soul, and the unbroken net shall be dragged to shore, "full of great fishes, one hundred and fifty and three."

"Sacrifice and offering Thou wouldst not: mine ears hast Thou opened: and I was not rebellious, neither turned I away back. Lo, I come to do Thy will, O my God; yea, Thy Law is within my heart, so I know that I shall not be ashamed."

OBEDIENCE LEADS TO THE DEEP.—Directly the Lord takes control, He steers towards the Deep. We no longer coast along the shallows, but begin to do business in great waters. "They that go down to the sea in ships, that do business in deep waters, these see the works of the Lord and His wonders in the deep." The Deep of the Eternal Council-Chamber, where we were chosen in Christ before the world began. The Deep of the Eternal Love, which loved us when we were yet sinners. The Deep of Fellowship and Unity with God, like that between the Father and the Son. The Deep workings of Providence which underlie all human history. The Deep Bliss of Eternity into which our restless souls will enter. The Spirit searcheth all things, even the deep things of God, and He will reveal them unto those that love Him.

But here we are specially concerned with *the Deep of Divine Partnership*. To Peter's surprise the boat, propelled by oar or sail, had passed over many well-known fishing grounds, and had kept its course to the midst of the lake, before our Lord bade them let down the nets. Immediately all hands were set to work, and the necessary preparations were hardly completed, when it was evident that they had netted a great shoal of fish. So much so that the nets were strained to breaking-point. The beads of perspiration were thick on his forehead, and his muscles stood out as whipcord, as Peter strove to cope with his spoils. His boat was lurching dangerously, and he made urgent signals for his partners, who apparently had put out in expectation that something of this kind would take place. And they came and filled both the boats, so that the gunwales were almost level with the water. Then Peter realized for the first time what partnership with Christ means, and how absolute obedience on our part secures absolute co-operation on His. Whilst the fishers were letting down their nets the Master had been issuing His mandate to the shoals of fish, which found themselves compelled by an irresistible impulse to make for the fishing-nets awaiting them. Was it not predicted in the eighth Psalm that this Son of Man should have dominion "over the fish of the sea, and whatsoever passeth through the paths of the Deep"?

What a lesson is here for us all! We know only too well what it is to toil through long dark seasons and take nothing. Again and again we have returned to shore with only a minnow or two. But directly we enter into fellowship, or partnership, with the Son of God, to which indeed we have been called, we discover that all we have to do is to have washed and mended nets, to trust the Master to indicate the grounds where the fish lie, and to believe that He will do all the rest. We may reckon absolutely on that co-operation of God. The Apostle says emphatically: "*God is faithful,* by Whom ye have been called into partnership with His Son."

On the Day of Pentecost Peter again let down his net, this time into the vast excited crowds, and again the Lord repeated the miracle of the Galilean lake, and filled his net with three thousand souls. In the house of Cornelius his net had hardly touched the water, when the shoal filled the net. "As I began to speak . . . the Holy Spirit fell." Surely on each occasion the Apostle must have looked into the face of Jesus with a happy smile, and said: "Ah! Lord, here is the Lake of Galilee over again."

This experience might be ours, on similar conditions. If it is not so, let us inquire for the reason. It lies, not with the Master, but with ourselves, our obedience, or our nets. If our nets are our addresses, sermons, or methods, we must make and mend them by careful study and earnest prayer. The meshes must be so closely articulated that no fish shall get through them. No pains should be spared so to present the Gospel as that our hearers may be without excuse. No vague and flimsy presentation of eternal truth is permissible. Mend your old nets, or make new ones.

Be sure also that they are clean. Wash out the sand-grit or weed that may have accumulated. Especially eliminate self. There must be nothing to attract your hearers from your message to yourself; and when you have done all, dare to believe that, though your Lord is now seated at the right hand of God, He is still working with His servants and confirming their word by the power of the Holy Ghost.

IV

A FISHER OF MEN

LUKE v. 8–11.

"I know not what I am, but only know
I have had glimpses tongue may never speak;
No more I balance human joy and woe,
But think of my transgressions and am weak."

Buchanan.

THE MASTER'S purpose for His disciples is disclosed in the words recorded by Matthew and Mark, and which were probably addressed to them on the shore, when they had again beached their boats: "Come ye after Me, and I will make you to become fishers of men." We can combine this form of the summons with that specially addressed to the impulsive, vehement, warm-hearted son of Jonas, and which is recorded in Luke v. It should be noticed that here, as generally in the Gospels, our Lord addresses him by the more intimate name of *Simon*, as though *Peter* were reserved till, through the months of discipline which awaited him, he was fitted to take the foremost place among his fellow-apostles.

The summons came whilst they were engaged in their usual occupation. David was summoned from the sheepfold to shepherd the chosen race. Paul was called from making the goat's-hair tents to teach the Church the ephemeral character of the things that are seen, in view of the House not made with hands, eternal in the heavens. The eternal springs were revealed to the woman as she rested her pitcher on the embrasure of Jacob's well. It was quite befitting, therefore, that our Lord should explain to his fisher friend the momentous and glorious ministry that awaited him, through the calling in which he had been engaged from boyhood, and which had so many points of resemblance with the work of winning souls. The one difference being brought out in the Greek word translated *catch,*

27

and which should be expanded to read, as in 2 Tim. ii. 26, "Thou shalt catch, *in order to keep alive*."

In every subsequent era sincere and earnest souls have lingered wistfully over these words, longing to extract from them the precious secret of successful soul-winning. More than two hundred years ago Thomas Boston, a young Scots Minister, made this record in his diary: "Reading in secret, my heart was touched with these words, *Thou shalt catch men*. My soul cried out for their accomplishing in me, and I was very desirous to know how I might follow Christ, so as to be a fisher of men; and for my own instruction I addressed myself to the consideration of that point."

It would be tedious to enumerate the various suggestions that have been made on the line of Boston's treatise, which was entitled, "A Soliloquy on the Art of Man-fishing." Many a godly minister with a perfectly-appointed Church, and surrounded by a devoted people—the boat, the company, and the fishing-tackle being all of the best—has watched, almost enviously, the success of some simple evangelist, who, apart from all adventitious aid, has lifted netfuls of fish from the great depths of human life into his creel. One expert fisherman says: "Keep yourself out of sight." Another urges that the bait and method must be carefully adapted to the habits of the fish. Yet a third insists on patience. What success is gained by scourging the water! All are good, but the study of this narrative may bring us still further into the heart of the matter and the mind of our Lord.

I. SUCCESSFUL SOUL-WINNING IS GENERALLY BASED ON A DEEP CONSCIOUSNESS OF PERSONAL SINNERSHIP.—Many instances present themselves from the biographies of the saints. But two will suffice. The untiring and extraordinary labours of the great Apostle of the Gentiles laid the foundations of the Gentile Church, but as he reviews the past and considers his natural condition, he does not hesitate to speak of himself as the chief of sinners and the least of saints. We faint not, he says, because the grace of God displayed its exceeding riches in our redemption. "We all once lived in the lusts of our flesh, fulfilling the desires of the flesh and of the mind, and were by nature children of wrath, even as the rest." John Bunyan's review of his condition, as it stood revealed in the light of God, is typical of many others, who shine as stars in the firmament of successful soul-winning. He says: "I was more loathsome in mine own eyes than was a toad; and I thought I was so in God's eyes also. I could have changed my heart with anyone. I thought none but the devil himself could equal me for inward wickedness and pollution of mind. I was both a burden and a terror to myself. How gladly would I have been anything but myself."

Those who have had deep experiences of the exceeding sinfulness of sin are the better qualified to be tender and pitiful to such as are sold under sin, are heaping up for then,selves agonies of remorse against the day of their awakening, are causing infinite sorrow to the Saviour, and are missing the great purposes for which they were created. "Alas, poor souls!" they cry, "such were some of us." The ringleaders in the devil's army make great soldiers for Christ. Their knowledge of Satan's stratagems and wiles is invaluable. Reclaimed poachers are notoriously the best game-keepers. The sinner knows the bitterness of the wages of sin, as an unfallen angel or an innocent child cannot. Men like Augustine or Bunyan have learnt by experience the subterfuges and evasions of conscience, the horror of remorse, the yearning for help. They are familiar with the holes where the fish lie, and the best methods of reaching them. They have infinite patience, as the Lord had patience with them. They bear gently with the erring, and with those who resent their approach, because they themselves have been compassed with infirmity. We are sometimes tempted to say with Augustine, *O beata culpa* (Oh, blessed fault!), because the knowledge of our own sinful hearts gives us the clue to all other hearts oppressed by temptation. We need not be surprised, therefore at this preparatory revelation of himself given to Peter.

He and the rest had known the Lord for at least eighteen months, but were unaware of His true majesty and glory. For them He was the carpenter of Nazareth, the holy man, the marvellous teacher and wonder-worker. That He was, like the Baptist, a chosen servant of God and the herald of a new era was their common conclusion. Beyond this their minds had not travelled. They regarded Jesus as of the same flesh and blood with themselves, felt glad to be honoured with His friendship, and were pleased in return to share with Him their slender stores or humble homes. It never occurred to them that they were in daily touch with the Lamb that was slain before the worlds were made, or that for their reception He had emptied Himself, made Himself of no reputation, and assumed the form of a servant.

Then most suddenly and unexpectedly this shaft of His essential being struck into their ordinary commonplace, and left a trail of supernatural glory. For a moment Peter was dazzled, almost blinded. He could hardly see for the splendour of that light; but as he felt the tug and pull of the bursting net, threatening to break beneath its sudden burden, he realized in a moment that his Teacher and Friend must have put forth a power which no mortal could wield. God was in the place, and he had not known it. How dreadful was that place! It was none other than the house of God and the gate of heaven; and at once the nakedness and sinfulness of his own heart were laid bare, and he cried: "I am a sinful man, O Lord." Note the significant exchange! When the boat left the shore it was *Master*, now, as this revelation has broken on him, it is *Lord*. Immediately on this Jesus said: "From henceforth thou shalt catch men."

There is a striking analogy between Peter's experience and Job's. The suffering patriarch had persistently and successfully maintained his integrity. "Till I die I will not remove mine integrity from me. My righteousness will I hold fast. I will not let it go. My heart shall not reproach me as long as I live." Then into his life God let fall visions of the Creation. He recited instance after instance of His almighty power, wisdom and skill. As Peter's eyes were unveiled that he might behold Christ's wonders in the deep, so were Job's; and he exclaimed, as the divine glory shone upon his soul, "I have heard of Thee by the hearing of the ear, but how mine eye seeth Thee, wherefore I abhor myself and repent in dust and ashes."

> *Oh agony of wavering thought*
> *When sinners first so near are brought.*
> *"It is my Maker!—dare I stay?*
> *My Saviour!—dare I turn away?"*

Whenever, therefore, this experience befalls, it may be deemed as preparatory to new success in soul-winning. Expect to hear the Lord answer your confession of lowly sinnership with a new summons to take your boat and net for a draught. And this experience does and will befall, not once or twice, but many times, as we approach nearer to the Alpine snows of our Lord's unsullied Holiness. The whole progress of the divine life within the soul is characterized by confessions. We are always being led to detect the presence of sin and evil in depths and motions, which once seemed comparatively harmless and innocent. The true soul is always counting its righteousnesses as filthy rags, and confessing that it has not yet attained nor is by any means perfect. The only confession that befits us is that we are following after to apprehend that for which we were apprehended of Christ Jesus. The higher the flight of the soaring eagle the deeper its reflection in the mountain-lake. Do not be afraid to know yourself beneath the Spirit's teaching, it is all preparatory to a new departure in "man-catching."

II. FAILURE AND SIN DO NOT NECESSARILY EXCLUDE FROM THE DIVINE PARTNERSHIP IN SOUL-WINNING.—"Depart from me," cried the conscience-stricken disciple. It was as though he said: "I will bring Thee, Lord, to the spot where I took Thee on board this morning; and when I have landed Thee, Thou must go Thy way and I mine. I shall ever love Thee and think of Thee as I float under these skies by day and night, but I am not fit to keep Thee company." And under his breath he may have whispered to himself: "But I know not how I shall live without Thee. To whom can I turn? Thou only hast the words of eternal life."

We can almost see him, when the well of the boat was heaped high with the slippery silver cargo, clambering across from prow and stern on his bare feet, falling at Jesus' knees as He sat near the tiller, clasping them, and faltering forth these words with the heaving sobs of a strong man torn with conflicting emotions.

It was as though our King Alfred, when wandering in Sherwood Forest, disguised, lost to his followers, and uncertain as to the path, had been found and befriended by a kindly woodsman, who had regarded him as an equal, shared with him his bed and board without detecting his royal dignity, and finally had conveyed him to his brave retainers. How startled he would be to see their deferential respect! Suddenly he would awake to the vast chasm intervening between himself and his ward, and approaching with many apologies for his familiarity, would deferentially propose to say good-bye and farewell for ever. "Our paths, sire, must of course diverge from this point! You to your throne, I to my cottage!" "Nay," said our Lord in effect, "that need not be. When sin is repented of, abhorred, and confessed, it need not debar from My presence or service. I can do with sinful men, who are conscious of their sinnership. No sin is too inveterate but that I can cope with it, too foul but that I can cleanse. Stay with Me, I will cleanse, heal, and save thee, and make thee the instrument of saving thousands of sinners like thyself."

It is impossible to exaggerate the comfort that these words afford to those who would fain serve Christ, though conscious of their profound unworthiness. "I am not worthy to bear the message of salvation to others, because I am such a sinful man! How canst Thou employ me, who hast hosts of unfallen angels at Thy command? How darest Thou identify Thyself and Thy holy cause with me? No, it cannot be! I love Thee, but an ever-widening river must divide us as we walk on either bank. I shall break my heart that I have failed Thee so, but I cannot lift up my face, or regain my forfeited place. Let me stand in the outer circle and see Thee now and again. I cannot ask for more, for Thou knowest, and I know, and every lost spirit knows, that I am a sinful man."

But Jesus has only one reply: "Fear not, from henceforth thou shalt catch men." "Fear not! I am the Daysman that stands as thy surety. I have blotted out thy transgressions as a cloud, and will no more remember thy sins. I have loved thee with an everlasting love, though I foresaw all this and more also. Depart from Me! It is unthinkable. Thou art dearer to Me than all the stars in their galaxies. I have obtained from the Father that thou shouldst be with Me, where I am. After thou hast had thy Pentecost, and fulfilled thy ministry and finished thy course, thou shalt be accounted worthy to stand in My Presence-chamber, that thou mayest behold My glory, and thou shalt share it."

"Lord, it is too much; let me kiss Thy feet!"

III. Soul-winning, to be successful, must be the Absorbing Purpose of Our Lives.—It cannot be one interest among many.

The Apostle said truly, "One thing I do." "They left all and followed Him." We can imagine that after this moving exchange of words Peter returned to his place to think over the marvel of the life that now opened before him. And whilst he mused, the fire burned. What else was worth living for? Surely he must obey this mandate. "Come ye after me!" "Hither, follow!"

May we indulge our imagination here? The boat responds to sail or oar, and makes for the shore. A friendly fisherman informs his wife that the well-known boat will soon be "in." His food has been waiting for him since early dawn. She had prepared a breakfast for which he did not come. She hastens to the shore and stands there with her welcome, all the gladder because she descries its burden. Her husband leaps into the shallow water and lifts Jesus from boat to beach. He then approaches her wistfully, and with an unwonted tenderness that startles her, "Can you spare me for a little?" he inquires. "The Master has asked me to go with Him. He says that I am not to fear, and that He will provide for us. He has promised to teach me how to fish for men. I will come back as soon as I have learned my lesson and He has done with me. In the meanwhile I must be free to serve Him. Can you spare me?"

And she replies: "Husband, go with Him. Mother and I will make shift somehow till you get back. Stay with Him as long as He needs you. Mother and I were saying only this morning that you have been a different man since you knew Him."

She came to believe also, and travelled everywhere with her husband, helping him, as Paul bears witness (1 Cor. ix. 5). We cannot suppose that Peter at once entered into the Master's passion for the souls of men. That was acquired afterwards. In the first instance he was content to follow *Him*, to listen to His words, to become His companion and helper. But it could not have been long before he and his companions began to be imbued with the same passion, until it became the master-motive of their existence.

So it will be with ourselves. As we walk with Christ, by the constant aid of the Holy Spirit, we shall be conformed to His image. His thoughts and yearnings will be transmitted to us by a Divine sympathy. We shall long to see Him honoured, loved, and exalted. We shall desire that He shall see of the travail of His soul and be satisfied. We shall become identified with His interests, and with no backward look on ourselves. The Holy Spirit will blow these sparks into a flame, and our life will be spent as that of Peter, who by his love for Christ was qualified to feed His sheep and lambs.

Let us ask that we may become partners with Christ in His great passion for men. Let us bring ourselves to this great magnet till we are magnetized. Oh to be a living flame for Jesus Christ, so that the uttermost love of woman may be:

Faint to the flame with which our breast is burning,
Less than the love wherewith we ache for souls!

V

PRIMER LESSONS

MARK i. 21–39.

"Sorrow is hard to bear, and doubt is slow to clear!
Each sufferer says his say, his end of the weal and woe;
But God has a few of us whom He whispers in the ear;
The rest may reason and welcome; 'tis we musicians know!"
                                                    Browning.

THE EPHESIAN Church was reminded by the Apostle of having been taught by the Lord Himself, "as the truth is in Jesus." It is therefore of extreme interest to study the earliest lessons with which our Lord commenced to prepare Peter and his friends for their life-work. Everyone who desires to be a soul-winner should sit in this lowest form in the Master's school.

THE FIRST LESSON WAS THAT ASSOCIATION WITH HIMSELF WOULD INEVITABLY INVOLVE THEM IN SPIRITUAL WARFARE.—It befell thus. On what was not improbably the first Sabbath after their final resolve to identify themselves with Jesus, the little group of fishermen, whose action was widely discussed all round the lake, giving them a considerable amount of notoriety, accompanied Him to the usual synagogue service. When the customary exercises were concluded, their Leader and Friend was invited to address the congregation, and as He proceeded in words of spirit and life to unfold the mysteries of the kingdom, the sharp contrast between His address and the dull deliverances of the Scribes to which they were accustomed struck them with astonishment. The contrast was as marked as between the sparkle of a waterfall and the stagnant water of a pit. "He taught them as one that had authority." Their hearts and consciences answered back with an echoing response.

The hush of the enthralled assembly was suddenly broken by the cry of a man's voice. It seemed as though a captive and unwilling

35

soul was made the organ of an alien and compelling spirit. "Let us alone," was the demand. "What have we to do with Thee, Jesus of Nazareth? I know Thee who Thou art:" This unclean spirit, or demon, may have tenanted that man's body and mind for years, unsuspected by his most intimate associates. But the near presence of the Divine Holiness, though curtained by the unrent veil of His flesh, extorted an involuntary but irresistible outcry. An inflamed eye may cause no special torture so long as it is screened from daylight, but expose it to a ray of meridian sunshine, and the anguish is too great to be endured. Ah! what will the unclean soul do when suddenly confronted in the other world by a glory before which unfallen seraphim veil their faces with their wings!

The disturbance caused by that wailing cry from the abyss must have been very startling. The man may, up to that moment, have been regarded as a respectable member of society. No one suspected the duality of his nature; but Peter must have suddenly realized that the type of character, for which his Master stood, dominated as it was by the Spirit of God, and essentially holy, must discover, arouse, and call into hostility the whole kingdom of evil spirits, which Christ afterwards described as the gates of hell, or Hades. The warfare for which he had enlisted was not against flesh and blood, but against the wicked spirits that rule the darkness of this world.

It was an infinite relief to know that his Lord was equal to the emergency. When He bade the unclean spirit to hold his peace and come out of this tormented nature, it could do no other than obey, though he convulsed his victim with malignant rage and cried again with a loud unearthly voice. The disciples shared in the general amazement, but they saw clearly—and our Lord was thankful that they realized—the necessity of a new apparatus of spiritual equipment. The weapons of their warfare would have to be spiritual, not carnal, or they would not be mighty enough to pull down these strongholds or emancipate the captives who all their life-time had been subject to bondage.

The scene in that synagogue gave Peter food for profound thought. He realized, as when a lightning flash illumines a midnight landscape, that there was a vast underworld of evil spirits—some of them probably fallen angels, and some wandering stars for whom is reserved the blackness of darkness for ever. He realized also that these would be violently perturbed, if any attempt were made to rescue their victims; that they had had some previous experience of the Lord in a state of existence known only to them and Him; that they were constrained to bear witness to His superlative Holiness; that they knew it must destroy them when the hour was struck by the clock of destiny; that, however much they strove against it, they could not resist His power; and that their one delight was to deceive and torture men.

It was not difficult for Peter to understand the effect produced on them by the Lord's Purity. He also had cried, only a few hours before, "Depart from me, for I am a sinful man, O Lord." But all his fear had passed, since he had yielded his will to obey and submitted to Christ's undisputed authority. The destruction which the demon feared in the disciple's case had wrought only for the destruction of the power of sin. The presence of Jesus for him and his brethren now meant joy unspeakable and full of glory. Thus he was being prepared to hear the Master say: "Heal the sick, cleanse the lepers, raise the dead, *cast out demons.* . . . Behold I give you power to tread on serpents and scorpions, and over all the power of the enemy, and nothing shall by any means hurt you."

THE SECOND LESSON WAS THE NEED FOR GENTLENESS IN MINISTRY.— Peter was strong, forceful, vehement. His voice would be loud, his tread heavy. His touch was not gentle enough for straightening bruised reeds. A considerable amount of training would have to be expended on him before he could commend, as he does in his epistles, compassion, pitifulness, and courtesy. It was necessary for him to *taste* that the Lord was gracious and to become clothed with that meek and quiet spirit, which is of great price (1 Pet. ii. 3; iii. 4, 8). The first lesson in this art was given in his own home.

After the amazing scene witnessed in the synagogue the Lord accepted the invitation of Peter and Andrew to come to the home, which they occupied in common, for rest and refreshment. James and John were included in the invitation. Probably some suggestion of this had been made previously, and the women of the household had been busily occupied in preparing. However, when the guests reached the door of the fishermen's home Peter's wife was on the outlook and taking him aside hurriedly whispered that her mother was down with "a great fever." She was lying on a couch in the inner chamber, with a dangerously high temperature. It may have been induced by her excitement to do all honour to their Guest. To outward appearance it was an unfortunate incident to occur on such a day! But untoward incidents, in the hand of Christ, become radiant memories.

"They told Him of her." Luke says that "they besought Him for her." But next to the marvel of her immediate recovery, so that she was able to take her part in ministering, they wondered at the tender gentleness with which the Master touched her hand, took her by the hand, and, as Peter subsequently dictated to Mark, raised her up. How little he realized that in after years he would do the same for a lame man on the Temple steps, and for the beloved Dorcas at Joppa.

The world needs tenderness as well as strength. Probably strength is never perfected until it is tender. The danger of modern philanthropy is that it does everything by rule and measure, in precise and strict adherence to a prescribed code, leaving no time or energy for the spontaneous workings of Christly tenderness. It is needed to touch the bleared eye of the blind, the seared flesh of the leper, and the feverish hand of a fever-stricken mother. Lives are blighted, homes are wrecked, and bright young hopes withered, for want of tenderness. But the child's hymn addressed to Jesus as the *tender* shepherd is exact in its epithet. He takes the lambs in His arms and carries them in His bosom, and gently leads those that are with young. Rockmen must combine tenderness and strength.

THE THIRD LESSON WAS A GLIMPSE INTO THE ANGUISH OF THE WORLD.—It had for long lain heavy on the Master's heart, and was constant incentive to the forth-putting of the saving strength of His right hand. Nothing less could sustain His disciples, and especially Peter, in all future trials and disappointments. It was therefore arranged that the fronts should be taken off the households of this one city, that their compassion might be moved by the vision of the anguish of a single community, although in fair and prosperous surroundings. All that were diseased and possessed, together with their agonized friends, were gathered at sunset in the humble street where Peter lived. He could not have believed that so vast a mass of misery and pain was concealed so near his home; but it was easier to pass from that heart-breaking spectacle to plumb the fathomless anguish of the world. The veil, which never intercepts the view from God, but which is drawn before our eyes lest life should be insupportable, was lifted for a few hours on that Sabbath evening whilst the stars came out one by one to watch sadly in heaven's vault.

The world is not all bad and sorrowful. Love, health, family life, children's laughter, the sweetness of living, must be valued at their true worth; but behind doors and windows there is a heavy makeweight of pain; and we need to know it, that, as with our Lord, so with His servants, we may sigh, as we look up, and say Ephphatha.

In the days of Esther none might enter the Persian court clothed in sackcloth. That is where kings go wrong. They refuse to recognize the sorrow and suffering which breed discontent and revolt. They insist that their papers shall be censored, and that all allusions to the sombre aspects of life shall be obliterated. No over-blown petals on their lawns, no dead birds in the wood, no lepers on the streets through which their chariot passes. "Sing songs," they cry, "clash cymbals, on with the dance, let mirth be unrestrained, give us unending pleasures, unsated amusement." So they have spoken, but foot by foot their throne has been compelled to give place to the ever-encroaching tide.

Not thus was it with the Lord. Whether it was a single leper or a crowd, He was always moved with compassion in the presence of human need. When Jesus beheld the multitudes, we are told, He was moved with compassion, because they fainted and were scattered abroad. We must needs learn this lesson, if we would win souls. The first, second, and third prerequisite for life-work, such as angels did for Lot and his family at the gates of Sodom, is to be filled with the merciful compassion that filled their hearts. The broken heart breaks and heals hearts!

The greatest of soul winners in any age avowed that he travailed in birth for his converts, and was willing to be accursed from Christ for his kinsmen according to the flesh. A speculum of ice may focus sunrays to a burning point, but cold hearts are not used of God to win lost souls. He preaches best who loves most. The height of the Nile on the Nilometer indicates the extent of the flood over the arid plains of Egypt and the subsequent abundance or failure of the harvest. If we are content to labour without conversions, we need not expect any. But if our soul breaketh with longing, or we can cry with Rebekah, "Give me children or I die," the answer will not tarry long. Blessed are they that hunger and thirst, for they shall be satisfied. Give us Thy tears, O Christ, as we behold the city! "Oh that mine eyes were fountains of tears, that I might weep day and night for the slain of the daughter of my people!"

THE FOURTH LESSON WAS AS TO THE SOURCE OF POWER.—In the early morning the household sought for their beloved and honoured guest, but the chamber was empty. In vain they searched the house. Where was He? The inquiry and search become general. "All men seek for Thee!" Perhaps a fisherman, who had returned at dawn from a night's fishing, informed them that he had met Him on the path that led to the silent hills above the town. Further up the slope a shepherd, who was preparing to lead his flock to the upland pastures, would indicate the sheltered dimple of the hillside, where the awe-struck search-party beheld the Master's kneeling or prostrate form. He had risen a great while before day and departed into a solitary place, where He prayed.

He could cast out demons and heal a crowd of sick folk, but (speaking after the manner of men) he was conscious of the ex-penditure of spiritual force. "He perceived that virtue had gone out of Him." His human nature required to be re-charged. Better leave some of the city-woe unredressed than forfeit that re-charging. Peter and his fellow disciples were destined to witness that spectacle many a time afterwards, until one day, when he ceased praying, one of them said: "Lord, teach us to pray."

Peter never forgot his Master's prayer habit, and he clearly determined to follow in those blessed footsteps. Pentecost came to him and the rest because they continued with one accord in prayer and supplication. The Sanhedrin was powerless to hurt because the whole company lifted up their voice to God with one accord. Prayer opened his way from his prison cell on the eve of execution. The vision of the Gentile world, cleansed and sanctified, was given as he prayed on the roof of the tanner's house.

Brethren, let us pray. Sisters, get on the mountain top and hold us up by your prayers, as we go down into the valley to fight. John

Wesley tells his preachers that their prime business is to win souls, and that only through unwearied labour and perseverance can they be free from the blood of all men, and he ends thus: "Why are we not more holy? Why do we not live for eternity and walk with God all the day long? Do we rise at four or five in the morning to be alone with God? Do we recommend and observe the five o'clock hour for prayer at the close of the day? Let us fulfil our ministry."

VI

THE SECOND PRIMER

LUKE iv. 1–13; JOHN vi. 1–21; MATTHEW xiv. 22–23.

" He might have built a palace at a word,
Who sometimes had not where to lay His head,
Time was, that He who nourished crowds with bread,
Would not one meal unto Himself afford.
Oh, self-denying love, which felt alone
For needs of others—never for it's own!"

Trench.

GOD'S Power in Nature awaits the use of any who will be wise and humble enough to study and obey the necessary conditions of its operation. The difference between the civilized and the savage races is largely that the former have learnt to avail themselves of the primal forces that hide in the flowing current, the wind, steam, electricity, or finally the ether; whilst the latter rely entirely on their agile or muscular limbs. Machinery is simply the cunning contrivance with which we endeavour to obey natural laws, with the inevitable result that the force behind them shall do our bidding. And there is no respect of persons. Whatever he may be, rich or poor, simple or learned, high-born or low-born, the son of a pauper or a monarch, he who desires Nature's co-operation can secure it, if he is prepared to pay the price of obedience to her inexorable conditions.

This is equally true of the operation of the Divine Spirit. He is prepared to co-operate with any who will faithfully fulfil His conditions. The poor, the weak, the despised, the nobodies of this world, can command and enjoy the greatest manifestations of the Divine energy equally with the cultured and refined. A turbine may drive a small sawmill or a big factory of spindles. Indeed, the simple and child-like dispositions can often make most of God, because they are most lowly and helpless in their self-estimate. Blessed are the poor in spirit for they are rich in faith, and heirs of the Kingdom.

It is therefore very necessary, not only for Apostles, but for us all, to learn the conditions on which spiritual power operates; and these are clearly set forth in the threefold temptation through which our Lord passed at the opening of His ministry. Let us adopt the order of the *Third* Gospel

1. *We must refuse to employ Divine Power for selfish uses. Then we may be trusted with it on behalf of others, and God will see to our needs.*

2. *True Rulership is won, not by conflict or force of arms, but by service, sacrifice, and suffering unto death.*

3. *Divine Power is granted, never for purposes of vainglory or ostentation, but for the help and blessing of others.*

The statement of these three principles may vary, but their essence is as invariable as Newton's law of motion. That Peter, the man of vehement force and energy, should become aware of them was especially needful, because in after-days he was to give witness with *great spiritual power* to the coming and glory of his Master and Lord. By an evident pre-arrangement of Divine Providence they were all compressed into experiences narrated by all the Evangelists, but especially in John vi.

I. TRUSTEESHIP FOR OTHERS DEPENDS ON THE DENIAL OF SELF.—At the given time and place, which had probably been prearranged, the Apostles gathered back to the Master, to tell Him what things they had done and taught. They needed an opportunity to discuss their recent experiences, to get guidance on their difficulties, and to share their joys. Almost immediately on their gathering back to Him the news reached them that John the Baptist—known, honoured, and loved by them all—had been treacherously murdered by the royal command in the dungeons of the Castle of Machærus, on the edge of the eastern desert. These rumours were confirmed by the arrival of his disciples, who had evidently feared the worst, had requested, not without peril to themselves, for the custody of the beloved remains, had buried them, and now had come to tell Jesus. It was clear that the tide of opposition was rising against the new movement. Wisdom suggested a temporary retirement from the public eye, and grief required seclusion in order to recover from the hurricane of desolation. It had quickly darkened the entire outlook, which had seemed so promising. "And He said unto them, Come ye yourselves apart into a desert (*i.e.*, an uninhabited) place and rest awhile: for there were many coming and going, and they had no leisure so much as to eat."

Entering the boat, they directed its course to the north-east corner of the lake, where the shore sloped up from the beach to a grassy plain of considerable expanse, and this in turn climbed to a noble forest of oaks. In the spacious amplitude of that sequestered spot were many glades and glens, where tired brains and sad hearts could be recuperated. The people, however, had noticed the course taken by the boat, and, hastening in a vast concourse round the head of the lake, presented an audience which appealed to Christ as the spectacle of a harried flock of sheep would appeal to the heart of a true shepherd.

Immediately our Lord subordinated all other considerations to the necessity of meeting the infinite need of more than ten thousand people. "He was moved with compassion, and healed their sick." ... "He began to teach them many things." But the most astounding experience of any was that which closed the day. With five barley-loaves and two small fishes, which Peter's brother, Andrew, had discovered in the wallet of a small boy—who with great pride and love had surrendered them, and whose faith perhaps afforded our Lord the human element which He always required—Jesus fed the whole vast crowd. "They did all eat, and were filled, and they took up twelve baskets full of the fragments and of the fishes."

Peter and the rest of the Apostles must have been fairly staggered by that experience. They could never forget it. Often, in after-days, when their simple story and appeal were used for the conversion of thousands, they would revert to this counterpart in the physical and material sphere. At the moment, however, they were confronted by the extraordinary contrast between their Master's poverty and His prodigal hospitality. He had told them that they were to take nothing for their journey, save a staff only. What was the good of a wallet, when there was no bread to put in it? They had also heard, probably from His own lips, the story of His forty days' fast, when He was tempted to use His power as the Beloved Son to turn the stones of the desert into bread. But evidently all the time He had the power of producing bread. Why had He not used it for His own need? Why had He not given them banquet upon banquet? Why did He sometimes in the early morning search a fig-tree on the road-side for a chance fig?

It seemed a strange paradox, but the paradox contained at its heart a vital truth. God will trust no one with His power who will use it for his own satisfaction and indulgence. We are tested in the wilderness by lonely hours, by long abstinence from the things that others crave and enjoy; and only when we have satisfactorily passed the test does God allow us to make full use of that power for the salvation and enrichment of others. This is the reason for the wilderness experience, which baffles and perplexes us. Is God angry with us? No! Has He forgotten to be gracious? No! Has He in anger shut up His tender mercies? No! Why, then, this desert? He is testing thee before He entrusts thee with the plenitude of His power. Meanwhile angels shall minister to thee at the end of thy forty days.

II. RULERSHIP DEPENDS ON SELF-GIVING.—After the meal the crowd seems to have been swept by a sudden impulse to make Jesus their leader in a determined revolt against their Roman oppressors. Here was a greater than Judas Maccabæus! The movement would be eagerly fostered by Judas of Kerioth and by Simon the Zealot. They had been waiting for this hour, and hoped to force Christ's hand. But He would have none of it. He had already fought this question out in the wilderness, when the devil had offered Him the kingdoms of this world and the glory of them. In that offer, as our Lord indicated in His interview with Pilate, there was an implication that force would be needed: "If My Kingdom were of this world, then would My servants fight." He swerved not by a hairbreadth of deviation from that great position. He knew only too well that the kingdoms of this world could never become His by force of arms, but at the price of agony and bloody sweat, of the Cross and Passion, and of the Death on Calvary.

He therefore first constrained His disciples to get into the boat, and put forth from the shore, whilst He sent away the people, with an authority that they could not dispute.   Then, retiring to the mountain solitudes, He (speaking after the manner of men) resolved that on the following day He would adopt a style of speech which would effectually shatter any further proposal of a carnal and worldly kingdom.

We shall have a further opportunity of considering this deliberate change in His policy; it is enough here to note how exactly the Master carried out the original programme formed as the Son of man on the threshold of his public career. What significance this lesson has for us all! It is not by the power of the secular arm, not by might nor by power, not by chariots and horsemen, not by the warrior host, the clash of steel, the victory of the battle or the forum, that the Church is to win her victory; but by service such as the Moravians gave to lepers; by sufferings like those of the martyrs in every age, not least in our own; by the sacrifice of tears and blood— the filling up of that which is behind of the sufferings of Christ—*thus*, *and only thus*, does the Kingdom come and is the Father's will done.

III. DIVINE POWER MUST NEVER BE USED FOR PURPOSES OF VAIN-GLORY OR DISPLAY.—"God will not give His glory to another." "That no flesh should glory in His presence." It is supposed by some that our Lord had appointed His disciples to meet Him at some well-known part of the coast, and that this made them toil so hard at the oar when presently the storm hurled itself down upon the lake. It may have been so, but it is not material to our present purpose. It is enough that He saw them toiling in rowing, and about the fourth watch of the night—*i.e.*, as the grey dawn began to spread through the stormy scene—"He cometh unto them, walking upon the sea." He used the water as the pavement of His approach. So often the storms that threaten us are permitted that we may learn to appreciate more truly the wonderful resources of His nature. When we take a course which His finger has clearly indicated the difficulties we encounter do not prove that we are wrong, but only that He has some fresh revelation to make of Himself. We can absolutely trust our Lord to take all the risks involved in our literal obedience to His will. "*Storms are the triumph of His art.*"

But Peter was animated by the spirit of adventure. It was not in him to remain quietly seated with all the others in the boat till the

Lord entered it. They might be satisfied with that quiescent welcome, but *he* felt that such an occasion called for some special departure on his part, a startling manifestation of love and faith, a conspicuous deed of splendid courage. There was a touch of vainglory and ostentation about it, of which he may have been unaware, though the Master descried it. When therefore Peter asked to be *commanded* to come to Him on the water, our Lord simply invited him to step out. He stepped forth, but his faith was imperfect, and he began to sink.

In the Lord's grave hour of temptation it had been suggested to Him that He should cast Himself down from the Temple portico to the depths of the valley, treading the air as Peter now attempted to tread the water. The Tempter had added the suggestion that angels would bear Him up in their hands, so that He should alight majestically and unhurt in the valley beneath. He had refused to act on the suggestion, because His Father had not so bidden Him. But there was another moment afterwards when He received from the Father the commandment to lay down His life, to breathe His soul forth in death, and descend the dark valley of shadow. As soon as He knew this to be His unmistakable duty, there was no symptom of hesitation; He became obedient to death, even the death of the Cross. And the everlasting arms of the Father bore Him down in His descent, that thence He might ascend far above all heavens.

There might come times in after-life when in like manner the clear command would come to Peter to step out of the boat of ordinary experience on to the storm-waves of persecution and martyrdom, but that hour had not yet come. He was not ripe for it then, nor afterwards when he rehearsed the same action with the same result in the hall of Caiaphas. His motives, which were now full of vainglory and self-confidence, must become purified and clear. Then it would not be needful to await the command to step out, because his duty would be unmistakable.

He began to sink. Though a good swimmer, he did not attempt to swim, but cried for help. Immediately the Lord's hand was stretched forth, and caught him, and they went together to the boat. No rebuke fell from those wise and gentle lips, except the question: "*Wherefore didst thou doubt?*" Obviously, one reason for his failure was that he watched the turbulence of the elements rather than the face and presence of his Lord. But there was a deeper reason for the failure. His faith was imperfect. There was a flaw in it. The slightest ingredient of self-hood invalidates faith's action, as Hawker's courageous effort to cross the Atlantic was spoilt by the collection of grains of silt in his filter. If you cannot avail yourself of God's promises, which are Yea and Amen in Christ, be absolutely sure that in some way the step you are making, and which you think to be good and right, is likely to fail, because, almost unconsciously, the element of pride, vainglory, boastfulness, or selfness is deteriorating your soul-life. Get rid of it by the incessant reference to the Cross. Mortify your soul-life, with its weak affections and strong desires. Say, with no bated breath, what our Lord said under similar suggestions: "Get thee hence, Satan; thou savourest the things of men, not those of God."

Thus Peter learnt the third lesson of his Second Primer; and it was with the undying impression of that hour that he wrote in after-days the notable advice: "Humble yourselves under the mighty hand of God, that He may exalt you."

"Cleanse, O Lord, we beseech Thee, the thoughts of our hearts by the inspiration of Thy Holy Spirit, that we may perfectly love Thee, and worthily magnify Thy Holy Name!"

> *"I have but Thee, my Father! let Thy Spirit*
> *Be with me still to comfort and uphold;*
> *No gate of pearl, no branch of palm I want,*
> *Nor street of shining gold."*

> *"Suffice it if—my good and ill unreckoned,*
> *And both forgiven through Thy abounding grace—*
> *I find myself by hands familiar beckoned*
> *Unto my fitting place."*

Whittier.

VII

TO WHOM, IF NOT TO CHRIST?

JOHN vi. 22–71.

" I watch them drift—the youthful aspirations;
Shores, landmarks, beacons drift alike!
Yet overhead the boundless arch of heaven
Still fades to night, still blazes into day
But Christ! my Christ! Thou wilt not drift away!"
Kingsley (altd.).

WHEN at last the crowds had dispersed, our Lord crossed the green-sward to the edge of the mountains, and began the ascent. His pulse quickened its beat, as ours does when we climb. The wild creatures darted from His path, not knowing Him. The sun descended to the western wave, and all the land was hushed and still, until the gathering storm reverberated through the funnels of the mountains and hurled itself on the lake. Did not that storm portend an even greater one, which, on the following day, was to break on the little band, who even then were fighting their way through the angry water?

A crisis was upon Him. He was becoming surrounded by a mixed crowd, who only desired to live on His bounty, and thought to exploit Him to gratify their wild passions for independence and revenge. He must clearly undeceive them, else they would wreck His great purpose of redemption, and make Him the tool of a political party. Immediate steps must be taken to arrest this movement. Not a day could be lost. On the morrow He would make such statements of the spiritual nature of His Kingdom as would effectually quench these incendiary sparks. Therefore, in fellowship with His Father, He gathered strength to disabuse His followers of their earthbound views. His mission was not to give meat and drink, but righteousness, and peace, and joy in the Holy Ghost. He knew quite well how much it would cost, but there was no alternative.

49

The following morning, on the farther side, witnessed a renewal of the excitement of the preceding evening, so our Lord withdrew into the comparative seclusion of the synagogue, and delivered that marvellous discourse of John vi., which, were it not for the further disclosures of Calvary, would be the high water-mark of the New Testament. And it changed the whole tenour of his career.

We are conscious of the added interest which characterizes the report of a speech, when successive parentheses record its reception by the audience. So in the Evangelist's narrative we can detect the effect which our Lord's deeply spiritual words had on the crowded audience. In verse 41 they murmured at Him. In verse 52 they strove among themselves. In verse 60 many, even His disciples, confessed aloud that His sayings were hard and difficult to be borne. In verse 66 many of those who had vowed their allegiance renounced Him, and quietly withdrew. "They walked no more with Him." By ones and twos, and then by groups, the crowd thinned away. First in order, the hot-headed politicians; then those who hoped for another meal; then the good-hearted but narrow-minded people who were shocked at His demand that they should eat His flesh and drink His blood, which, even if it were taken spiritually, arrogated for the speaker the claims of Deity. Finally, the synagogue was entirely emptied, except for the little group of aghast Apostles who had been the sorrowful witnesses of the shattering of the Master's popularity and of the fabric of their private ambitions. It was then that He looked round on them and put the pathetic question, "Will ye also go away?" which drew from Peter the unhesitating reply: "Lord, to whom shall we go? Thou hast the words of Eternal Life, and we have believed and know that Thou art the Holy One of God."

I. THE URGENCY OF THE QUESTION.—To whom shall we go? The question presses on us, as on Peter. He knew something of the ritualism of the Pharisee and the dogmatic negations of the Sadducee, of the wild mythologies of the Greeks, and the crass materialism of the Romans. Perhaps some slight knowledge of the mystic speculations of the Orient had floated in on the shores of the lake with the merchandise of India or China. But what comfort and help did any one of these various systems, traditions, or philosophies, yield to a world or a soul weary to the point of exhaustion and sick with sin?

Peter knew that the soul of man must go somewhere. It must needs go outside itself for living water and satisfying bread. There had awoke within his soul cravings for the eternal, the infinite, and the divine. He had known nothing of these in earlier days, which seemed so far away, before the voice of the Baptist had rung out its clarion appeal and startled his slumbering soul. But since he had awoke to the realities of the spiritual world, all former sources of inspiration and instruction had failed to satisfy. He was henceforth conscious of an inward cry like that of the Psalmist: "My heart and my flesh cry out for the living God." That cry, as Peter knew by profound inner experience, could be answered only by his Lord. To whom else could he go?

To whom shall we go at this time of world-weariness? Men have tried every system of human government, every phase of human philosophy, every form of religious cult. Like a restless sleeper, they have tossed restlessly on their beds and beneath their coverlets; but the one is shorter than a man can stretch himself on it, and the other narrower than a man can wrap himself in it. "Many there be which say, who will show us any good?" Suicide is said to be on the increase. Immorality and the laxity of the marriage tie suggest the wane of love, and hope, and faith. The clouds of revolution and searching trial are hurrying up the sky. Ancient landmarks are being swallowed by the advancing tides of change. This is the predicted hour of trial—"the hour which is to come upon the whole inhabited world, to try them that dwell upon the earth." To whom shall we go?

To whom shall we go when our souls have suddenly awoke to the majesty of the Eternal Presences, which are hidden by the glare of pleasure, but emerge in hours of loneliness, change, sorrow, and loss?

To whom shall we go when in the light of the great white throne we suddenly find that snow-water can never cleanse hearts and consciences, on which sin has laid its defiling hand?

To whom shall we go when one by one the lights which we have trusted die out in the sky, and neither sun nor stars shine for many days, and no small tempest lies upon the distraught soul, which hears the breakers dashing on an unknown shore?

To whom shall we go in the loneliness of age, in the pains of mortal sickness, in the hour of death, in the day of account, amid the splendour of a holiness which angels cannot face, and a purity before which the heavens are not clean?

Peter had every warrant for his inquiry. It expresses the agonized cry of the human, when the divine and eternal have broken in upon its insensate stupor.

II. THE ALTERNATIVES TO CHRIST.—Let us understand clearly what we want. We want Life, Eternal Life, the pulse and throb within our systems of something beyond emotion, affection, intellect, or reason, and which shall be to our spirit what physical life is in our daily experience. "'Tis life, of which our souls are scant."

Jesus awakens mysterious longings in our souls. We cry and fret, as a child that awakes suddenly in an empty room and weeps. Plato said that these were reminiscences of a former life, when the soul was perfect in a perfect heaven. Wordsworth would say that they are glimpses of that immortal sea which brought us hither. We are indifferent to their origin; we only know that we turn from the vanities of the world's satisfaction, as beasts from tainted wells.

Shall we go to the sceptic? He will deride our demands, as the phantasies of disordered minds. It is as though one were to assure a hungry man that the sense of hunger was an absurd mistake.

Shall we go to the ritualist? He will offer us rites, which, though fragrant with all that satisfies our sense of beauty or gratifies our reverence for the past, are inadequate to quench the soul's passion for the living God and allay the fever of remorse.

Shall we go to the great religions of the East? Has Confucius, or Buddha, or Mohammed, or the ancient Vedas, a medicine for the soul, that has seen in Christ the Holy One of God, and in whom the Spirit of Christ has started infinite desires for assured forgiveness, for acceptance with God, for the white robes of purity, and the talisman of victory over inbred corruption?

Try every door! Each opens on despair; on the sea moaning at the foot of the cliffs. You hear its ceaseless chafing, you can just descry the foam of the remorseless breakers. But it is night.

There is no satisfaction but in Christ. "The depth saith, It is not in me; and the sea saith, It is not with me. It cannot be gotten for gold, neither shall silver be weighed for the price thereof. It is hid from the eyes of all living and kept close from the fowls of the air."

But Jesus said: "I thank Thee O Father, Lord of heaven and earth, that Thou didst hide these things from the wise and understanding, and didst reveal them unto babes. Yea, Father, for so it was well-pleasing in Thy sight."

III. THE IMPERISHABLE SUPREMACY OF JESUS.— His teaching—or "words," as Peter put it—are diametrically opposed to the bent of human nature. They were opposed to the Jewish exclusiveness on the one hand, and the Gentile culture on the other. But He never sought to gain adherents by lowering His claims. He made no concessions to the passions or prejudices of His hearers. Though His human nature craved for sympathy and faith, He stood as a rock in unwavering steadfastness to His great ideals. What has been the result? This, as Napoleon precisely stated it: "Whilst great empires created by human genius have sunk in ruins, millions have died for Christ, and millions would gladly die again." And what are the grounds of His imperishable supremacy?

Though All-Holy, He satisfactorily deals with the grave question of sin. Sin is a terrible reality to the awakened soul. It drives the fakir to horrible self-torture. It has covered the earth in every age with altars and priests. It has extorted from the saintliest books of bitter confession. It has been the energizing cause of religious movements that have moved the world. Men have ridiculed its introspections and expressions as "the mumps and measles of the soul." They have sought to ignore and stifle it. They have suggested palliatives. Jesus alone has put sin away, has satisfied the sense of justice and the plea for mercy, and has supplied from His Blood and Righteousness the one all-satisfying answer to the inquiry, "Can God forgive me righteously?"

Though Man in His Incarnation, He communicates and is the Bread of God. Bread furnishes to our digestions the influences which the corn-plant has absorbed from sun and earth, from the kisses of the summer and the dews of the dawn, from the mysterious actinic rays of light and the silent brooding of the night. Similarly, our Lord brings to us the wealth of the Eternal and Infinite God in such a manner that His words of life, and the living presence of the Spirit in our hearts, convey to our receptive natures that Eternal Life which was with the Father before all worlds, and was manifested to

Peter and the rest and through them to the world. We know that bread nourishes us. It is a daily experience. No amount of argument or chemical demonstration could make us more sure than we are by habitual practice. So with our Lord. We know and are sure, because we have handled, tasted, and felt.

Though there is mystery in His words which repels the superficial, that very mystery is an additional reason for our faith. They go away because they do not understand. But we are attracted because, though we do not understand, we find that there is a fitness in the mystery of our own profound experience being met by an equal mystery in Him. A Christ whom we could absolutely fathom, measure, diagnose, weigh, and analyse, would be no Christ for us. We are sensible of desires for joy unspeakable, peace that passeth understanding, and love that passeth knowledge; and we find Him always before us. Deep calls unto deep. The deep of our nature finds a response in the deep of His. He satisfies. He does better for us than we can ask or think. For brass He brings gold, and for iron silver, and for wood brass, and for stones iron. He is always leading to fresh fountains of water of life. Eye hath not seen nor heart conceived what He has in store for those that love. Oh, my heart, with thy heights and depths, and insatiable longings, thou hast found more than thy match in Jesus! To whom else canst thou go?

For private prayer, it is an admirable custom to pass in thought through the spiritual counterpart of the Tabernacle or Temple of old. To renew our consecration at the Altar, to wash in the Laver, to light again our love at the burning Lamps, to offer our intercessions at the golden altar of incense—all is good; but we must see to it that we eat of "the bread of God" on the Table of Incarnation before we enter with boldness into the Holiest of All through the Blood of Jesus.

VIII

"I GIVE UNTO THEE THE KEYS"

MATT. xvi. 13–20.

"A poor man served by thee shall make thee rich;
A sick man helped by thee shall make thee strong;
Thou shalt be served thyself by every sense
Of service which thou renderest."

E. B. Browning.

FOR TWO years and a half our Lord had lived amongst His Apostles. Making Himself of no reputation, He had given them no certain clue to His dignity. The Prince had never thrown aside his incognito. It was not for Him to blazon forth his attributes, but to live a life, the like of which had never before been seen by human eyes. To quote the words of His evangelist and friend, who more than any other penetrated beneath the Lord's grace and truth to their hidden fountain—"The life was manifested, and we have seen it."

Only six months of education remained before He was taken from them—a period during which His teaching must become much more intensive; and as a preliminary it was necessary to ascertain what conclusions they had arrived at, as the result of their observations and experiences. If, notwithstanding His reticence, they had discovered His intrinsic glory, "the glory of the Only-Begotten of the Father," it would serve as the common platform from which to ascend to higher revelations. But if, on the contrary, the god of this world had succeeded in blinding their eyes to His glory as the image of God, it would be clear that they could not serve the high purpose of His calling, and that He must go elsewhere for the heralds of His Gospel and the foundation stones of His Church.

In order to secure the necessary privacy for this all-important inquiry, our Lord journeyed to the extreme edge of the northern frontier of Palestine, where Mount Hermon, the chief Alp of the

Lebanon range, lifts its mighty mass beyond the snow-line, screening off the northern blasts, and cooling the air, so that the dews of Hermon descended on the mountains of Zion. The Jordan issues from one of the cliffs near the ancient town of Banias, known at that time as Cæsarea Philippi—a conjunction of the names of the Emperor and the local ruling kinglet. There the little band found lodgings, and we can imagine the blessed intercourse which ensued on the verdant slopes of the foot-hills, or in the glens and glades of the ancient cedar-forests. These were the worthy setting of the memorable conversation, which more than any of our Lord's discourses has affected the life of Christendom.

I. THE MASTER'S SEARCHING QUESTION.—"Whom do men say that I the Son of man am?" The answers were various. It was universally acknowledged that He was no ordinary man. People felt that a Divine fire was burning beneath the pure porcelain of His nature. But their views were as various as the speakers. Some, with Herod at their head, expressed the belief—not without a shudder— that the Baptist had risen from his lonely grave beside the Castle of Machærus. Others said that Elijah, whom Malachi had taught them to expect, had come to them in the "day of the Lord." Others traced a resemblance between Jesus and one of the old prophets. Probably our Lord was not specially disappointed or surprised by these replies. It was of small importance what conclusions had been arrived at in the Court of Public Opinion. He knew what was in man; and these inquiries were only intended to lead up to the second and all-important question: "But whom say ye that I am?"

Speaking after the manner of men, his heart must have stood still for the reply. And it came instantly, emphatically, and decisively from the lips of Peter, always the spokesman for the rest: "Thou art the Christ, the Son of the living God." This was a great advance on the earlier confession of John vi., as it appears in the Revised Version. In a most significant manner it combined the hope of the Jew for the Anointed One, with the recognition of the unique and essential nature of our Lord, as the Only-begotten of the Eternal God. It filled the heart of Jesus with ecstasy. The bluff fisherman had been taught the secret of the mystery which in other ages had not been made known unto the sons of men, as it was now to be revealed to the holy Apostles and Prophets by the Spirit. "Blessed art thou, Simon Bar-Jona (son of Jonas or John), for flesh and blood hath not revealed it unto thee, but My Father which is in heaven." These words sometimes make us wistful. Oh for these flashes of spiritual intuition! Oh for this insight into the Divine mysteries! Oh to know even as we are known! Hush, soul! "The secret of the Lord is still with them that fear Him." The Spirit of the Father still speaks in human hearts in gentle whispers, as once in Horeb's cave. "It is written in the Prophets, And they shall be all taught of God." Every man therefore that cometh unto Christ hath heard and hath learned of the Father. Even we may receive, not the spirit of this world, but the Spirit which is of God, that we may know "the deep things of God."

II. THE FOUNDATION OF THE CHURCH.—Then for the first time our Lord spoke of His Church. Notice the strong possessive pronoun *My*. As yet the Church—one, undivided, and hidden—existed only in the councils of eternity. The future tense, "I *will* build," makes it clear that as Eve was builded out of Adam whilst he slept, so the Church was presently to be built from the death-wound and the sepulchre entombment of Emmanuel. And it was destined to be His bride, His body, His fulfilment, through which He could manifest the complete lory of His nature. *My* Church! From eternity Christ loved her. By His blood He redeemed her. Through His Spirit and by His Word He is cleansing her; and one day He will present her to Himself a glorious Church, "having neither spot, nor wrinkle, nor any such thing." As the good steward, Eliezer, brought Isaac's bride from a far country, so the Holy Spirit is completing the Church in these last days, and preparing her to be for ever with the Lord.

The Church is the special object of hatred to the dark underworld of fallen spirits, whom our Lord refers to as "the gates of Hades." Hades is the nether unseen world, the abode of the wicked spirits that rule the darkness of this world, under the leadership of "the P ince of the power of the air," who rules in the hearts of the disobedient. The gate, in Oriental thought and speech, was the place for council, judgment, the connivance of stratagems and the mustering of hostile forces. Our Lord clearly anticipated the long and weary conflict that would be inaugurated against His Church. "And the dragon was wroth with the woman, and went to make war with the remnant of her seed, which keep the commandments of God, and have the testimony of Jesus Christ." Yes, and the Church can only overcome "by the blood of the Lamb," and by "the word of her testimony." Her children love not their lives unto the death!

Long and sore the conflict may be, but the issue is not doubtful. "*They shall not prevail.*" "The Lamb shall overcome, for He is Lord of lords, and King of kings, and they that are with Him are called, and chosen, and faithful." There shall break ere long on the ear of a startled world the voice of a great multitude, which in the distance shall sound like the voice of waves breaking on the shore in a summer night, but nearer their words of victory shall be distinctly audible, as they announce—first that the Church has emerged victorious; and, second, that the Marriage of the Lamb has come, and His Bride has made herself ready. The secret of the Church's prevalence over her foes consists in her foundation doctrine. Shall we not rather say, her foundation *fact?* Not the personality of an impulsive and fallible man, who within a few moments was to incur the sharpest rebuke ever administered by those gentle lips; but the Deity of our Lord, as "the Son of the ever-living God." The Greek phrasing of our Lord's reply leaves no doubt as to His meaning. Two Greek words are here. *Petros*, Simon's new name, signifying in Greek, as Cephas did in Syriac, a stone, or bit of rock, broken or hewn from its parent bed; and *Petra*, the Rock-bed itself. Our Lord carefully makes the distinction. If He had intended Peter to be the foundation of the Church, He would naturally have shaped His sentence thus: "Thou art Peter, and on *thee* I will build My Church." But carefully selecting His words, He said: "Thou art Peter, a stone, a fragment of rock, who under the power of God's Spirit hast spoken with strength and certainty; but I cannot build on thee, for the foundation of My Church I must turn from Petros to Petra, from a fragment to the great truth, which for the moment has inspired thee. The truth of My eternal relationship to the Father is the only foundation, against which the waves of demon and human hatred will break in vain. No stone shall give. No bastion shall even rock."

III. THE GIFT OF THE KEYS.—It must be carefully noted that our Lord used the same words which He addressed to Peter also to individual believers in Matt. xviii. 18, and again to His assembled Apostles *and others* who were gathered with them in the Upper Room on the evening of the Resurrection Day. See Luke xxiv. 33, and John xx. 22 and 23.

In the light afforded by these references we may extend the significance of this gift of the keys to include all who live and act in the power of the Holy Spirit. If we have received that blessed gift of the Comforter, as they did on whom the Master breathed that Easter evening, we also may wield the power of the keys. Not ours the prerogative of the Apostles, but only the humble distinction of having walked to Emmaus, first with broken and then with burning hearts; yet even such may, in the power of the Spirit, be entrusted with keys that shall open closed doors, and emancipate prisoners from their cells.

Here, for instance, is a broken-hearted penitent who thinks that her sin is too great to be forgiven, and some Christian sister takes as her key our Lord's words to such in Luke vii. or John viii., and instantly a door is opened by which she passes into the Peace of God.

Again, there may be a man who thinks that he is guilty of the unpardonable sin, and a scribe, who is well instructed in the mysteries of the Kingdom, takes as his key the words spoken by our Lord under similar circumstances: "All sins shall be forgiven unto the sons of men"; and making a distinction between sins and the condition of absolute deadness and insensibility into which men may drift, when they have killed their conscience, so that it no more remonstrates or pleads, he opens the door into the liberty of the sons of God.

Again, there may be the case of a morbid and unhealthy conscience, which is bound by scruples and tormented by questions, and you may take as your key Col. ii., or Gal. iii. and iv., and instantly the wards of the prison lock yield, the door opens, and the captive, like Peter touched by the Angel, passes through the gate that leads out into the City of the Firstborn.

This is the secret of the quest of the blessed life. Go through the world opening prison-doors, lifting heavy burdens, giving light, and joy, and peace to the oppressed, proclaiming the Lord's Jubilee year. Shut doors opening out on the dark waters of despair. Unlock and open those that face towards the sunrise. For this is work that angels might envy. "Receive ye the Holy Ghost."

The Knights of Arthur's Table rode forth into the wild wastes of the Kingdom of the Beast, intent on righting wrong, and succouring the oppressed. Never a day without its gallant deed. We, too, are dedicated to similar enterprise. Let us not hold back lest we miss the vision of the Holy Grail! We, too, possess the Sword of the Spirit and the Keys of the Kingdom! We, too, may catch a glimpse of the holy cup of sacrifice!

IX

"WITH HIM ON THE HOLY MOUNT"

MATT. xvii. 1–9; 2 PET. i. 16–18.

"If ever on the mount with Thee
I seem to soar in vision bright,
With thoughts of coming agony,
Stay Thou the too presumptuous flight.
Gently along the vale of tears
Lead me from Hermon's sunbright steep,
Let me not grudge a few short years
With Thee toward Heaven to work and weep."
Keble.

ON THE afternoon of the last day of our Lord's sojourn at Cæsarea Philippi He proposed to His three chief Apostles that they should accompany Him for a season of retirement to the upper slopes of Hermon. Little realizing what awaited them, they readily consented, and accompanied Him to a scene which left an ineffaceable impression. In his last days Peter referred to it as affording the outstanding evidence of his Master's Divine nature and mission. For him it was "the Holy Mount," where he and the others had been eye-witnesses of Christ's majesty, when He received from the Father honour and glory. There could be no doubt about it. They had not followed nor promulgated cunningly devised fables!

I. THE ACCESSORIES OF THE TRANSFIGURATION.—*The place was clearly Mount Hermon.* The previous days had been spent at its foot. Mount Tabor, which formerly was supposed to have been the chosen spot for this sublime spectacle, was at that time (so later investigation has proved) the site of a Roman fort and garrison, which would have been totally incongruous with the mystic beauty of heavenly glory. And the vivid comparison, in Peter's special Gospel of Mark, between the Master's appearance and the snow, is an additional confirmation that Mount Hermon's snow-capped heights were in his thought. Here only in Palestine is'there the permanent presence of snow. *The time was almost certainly the night.* Our Lord was accustomed to spend nights on the mountains, which are the natural altars of the world. The overpowering sleep that mastered the Apostles, until the Transfiguration Glory was on the point of passing, also suggests the night season. This conclusion is further corroborated by the fact, as we are expressly told, that it was "the next day" when they came down from the hill and met the excited crowd, which had been attracted by the poor demon-possessed boy and his demented parents. We need not dwell on the enhanced beauty which is shed on the entire narrative by the reflection that the background of the night afforded additional beauty and lustre to the radiant glory which enwrapt the Person and garments of the Lord.

It is noticeable that the glory passed on Him as He prayed. In the case of Moses the glory of his face was due to its absorption of the Eternal Light on which he gazed. It was a giving back of what had been received. There are diamonds which, after being held in the sparkle of the sun, will continue to coruscate long after they have been transferred to a darkened chamber. Moses had spent forty days and nights in God's presence-chamber, and the light before which Israel shrank away was the immediate result of that memorable interview. As he beheld he was changed into the same image. But in the case of our Lord the glory which the disciples beheld—which streamed through His garments, so that His ordinary dress became shining, exceeding white as snow, so as no fuller on earth could whiten—was the raying forth from within of the glory of the Only-begotten of the Father. It is not improbable that, whenever He was alone on the mountain heights in fellowship with His Father, He laid aside His shrouding disguise, and the same phenomenon recurred, though there were no eye-witnesses to chronicle it.

In this connection let us heed the earnest beseeching admonition of the Apostle Paul, who had only heard of the Transfiguration during his memorable fortnight spent, years after, with Peter. Let us be transfigured by the renewing of our minds; then, as we present our bodies as a holy and living sacrifice to God, they also shall be transfigured—the light shall shine from within and prove what is the good and acceptable and perfect will of God.

The appearance of Moses and Elijah added greatly to the impressiveness of the spectacle. They were the representative leaders of the Hebrew Theocracy. Moses was the embodiment of the Law, Elijah of the Prophets. In both cases the circumstances of their removal from the scenes of earthly ministry had been remarkable. Moses had died on the lonely heights of Pisgah beneath God's kiss, and was buried by His hands in an unknown grave. Elijah had gone home in a chariot of fire, sent for his convoy. But these wonders did not account for their advent, which was due to the special encouragement which they were able to afford the Redeemer at this great crisis.

Only a few days before our Lord had unfolded, with graphic minuteness, the scenes of His approaching death. Immediately Peter, speaking for the rest, had sought to dissuade Him. "Spare thyself," he said; "this shall not be for Thee." They were not able to understand or sympathize. Love, doubtless, and passionate devotion inspired this impulsive soul in taking on himself to rebuke his Lord. But, as on the Mount afterwards, so then, he knew not what he said. It was necessary, therefore, that redeemed humanity should furnish two of its strongest and noblest ambassadors to reinforce and strengthen our Lord, upon the human side, ere He set His face steadfastly to go up to Jerusalem to die. He was acting on the agreement of the Eternal Council-chamber, and pursuing the course marked out before the foundation of the world; but, as in the glades of Gethsemane an angel was sent to strengthen His human nature, so now Moses and Elijah were the chosen emissaries of the Eternal World, who stood on His right and left, assuring Him of the Father's sustaining help, and of the glory which must accrue when the bitterness of death had passed.

II. THE THEME OF THE CELESTIAL VISITANTS.—"They spake of the *decease* which He was to accomplish at Jerusalem." The Greek word is "exodus"—a term which struck Peter's imagination. In after years he employed it of his own death. "I must put off this tabernacle," he said, "even as our Lord Jesus Christ hath showed me; but I will endeavour after my exodus that you may have these things always in remembrance."

It must have been a very startling rebuke to Peter and his companions. To them the death of the Cross seemed as unthinkable as it appeared unnecessary. Certainly He who had saved others could save Himself from such incredible shame and torture! Surely it must never take place! Neither God nor man could suffer it! Their Lord might have incurred the hatred of their religious leaders, but there need be no collision between Him and the Roman authorities, and these alone could impose death by crucifixion.

But now, to their surprise, they discovered that Heaven could speak of nothing else! It was apparently the one subject about which Moses and Elijah cared to speak. Whatever their differences in character and function, they were in absolute agreement on this all-absorbing topic. As soon as the opportunity offered of intercourse with Jesus, they fell to talking on it. It was the absorbing theme that engrossed the innumerable company of angels and the spirits of just men made perfect. The songs of the celestial harpers were set to this key-note, and the angels were bending over the mystery of a world's redemption, as their Lord drew nearer to paying its price, not with silver and gold, but with precious blood, as of a lamb without blemish and without spot. He had been fore-ordained before the foundation of the world, but was now about to manifest the uttermost of Divine Love, in the last times of the Hebrew dispensation.

Moses would speak of the Passover Lamb, the slaying of which preceded the Exodus by which his people passed to liberty, and would assure our Lord that His death would mean emancipation and victory, when—on the shores of the sea of glass, its placid waters red with the mingled fire of the Eternal Sunrise—the ransomed hosts of the redeemed would sing the song of Moses and the Lamb.

Elijah would remind Him that the spirit of prophecy was the testimony of Jesus, and that it was written in the Prophets and the Psalms that the Christ should suffer and should enter into His Glory. He would specially quote Isa. liii., that He should see of the travail of His soul and be satisfied, and that by His knowledge He should justify untold myriads.

Moses would testify that each victim which had bled on the altars of Israel had no intrinsic virtue to put away sin; and that if He were now to fail, all their suffering would be abortive, and that the redemption which the saints were already enjoying must be revoked.

Elijah would assure Him that on the other side of the Jordan of death, the strong waters of which He would cleave as He passed, the chariot of the Ascension cloud awaited Him. He might have said: "By death Thou wilt abolish death. Thou wilt rob death of its sting and the grave of its victory. Thou wilt bring Life and Immortality to light. The waters of Jordan will be cut off for ever, and all Thy redeemed shall pass over on dry land."

Clearly, the death of the Cross, which our Lord saw awaiting Him on the sky-line, is the theme of Eternity. At first the holy beings celebrated in ceaseless chant the story of Creation: "Worthy art Thou, our Lord and our God, to receive glory and honour and power, for Thou didst create all things." But this was latterly exchanged for the yet more jubilant outburst: "Worthy is the Lamb." He was the Lamb slain before the foundation of the world. The effect of His death was destined to be felt, not only on earth, but in reconciling things in the heavens. Every created thing which was in heaven and on the earth and under the earth, and on the sea, and all things that were in them, were to be affected by it, and probably brought nearer the heart of God. Because He would become obedient to the death of the Cross, every knee would bow to Him, and every tongue confess that He was Lord, to the glory of God the Father. He would obtain the Name that was above every name; would put down all rule, authority, and power; and would win the subjection of all things to Himself, preparatory to handing all to the Father, that He might be All in all! Can we wonder at the intense interest with which the great cloud of witnesses watched the Saviour, as (so to speak) He stepped into the stadium to run the last lap in the great race, to fight the last fight in the stupendous struggle? The battlements of the Holy City were crowded with awestruck crowds, until the Ascension hour called them to follow in the glad procession of the Victor. Without controversy, great is the mystery of Godliness. He was manifest in the flesh, justified in the Spirit, seen of angels, preached among the Gentiles, believed on in the world, received up into glory.

III. THE ENFOLDING CLOUD.—Peter had made a suggestion, which was as ill-considered as it was hasty. In his account of this scene, communicated through Mark, he admits that he knew not what he was saying. It was a preposterous suggestion, which at least would make the Crucifixion impossible, that our Lord should disregard the claims of a lost world, and spend His remaining years in a tabernacle on the mountain-side. According to Peter, Moses and Elijah were also to be detained from their blessed residence and ministry in the Upper Sanctuary. To think of these six living in rapturous fellowship on a high mountain-top, instead of coping with such scenes as that which awaited at the mountain-foot! Peter had much to learn, and far to travel ere he could write: "Who His own self bare our sins in His own body on the tree, that we, being dead to sins, might live unto righteousness; by whose stripes ye were healed."

Whilst he was speaking thus he and his fellow Apostles beheld a cloud descending, which enveloped the radiant vision. They feared as they saw their Master and His celestial visitants cut off from them and hidden in the brightness of that mist of glory. "Behold a bright cloud overshadowed them." It was no ordinary cloud, but was probably the Shekinah-cloud that led the wilderness march, that filled Solomon's Temple on its dedication, and that formed the Lord's Ascension Chariot. From its heart the voice of the Eternal God was heard, bearing sublime witness to the Saviour as the Beloved Son, and demanding homage from all. That voice was heard by the three awe-struck Apostles, and surely their solemn attestation to this remarkable testimony is full of re-assurance and confirmation.

What might have been! As the sinless Man, the Second Adam need not have died. Had the first Adam not sinned, he would probably have passed to God, as those will who are alive and remain to the Coming of the Lord. So with Christ, the sinless Man. His mortality might have been swallowed up of life. He need not have been unclothed, but clothed upon. In a moment, in the twinkling of an eye, He might have passed with Moses and Elijah, through the open door of Paradise, to become the Patron, though not the Redeemer, of our race. Such a translation might have been possible; but if, at any moment, it was presented to His mind, He thrust it away, as He did when Peter suggested it, with, "Get thee behind me, Satan, thou savourest the things of men." For the joy that was set before Him—

or instead of the joy set before Him—He turned his back on Paradise for Himself, that He might open Paradise for the dying thief and for us. And when the cloud had passed, He was left alone with his Apostles, and took the straight road to Calvary. In the words of Isaiah, He set His face like a flint, and we know that He has not been ashamed!

X

"FOR ME AND THEE"

MATT. xvii. 24–27.

"Away despair! my gracious Lord doth hear.
Though winds and waves assault my keel,
He doth preserve it; He doth steer,
Ev'n when the boat seems most to reel.
Storms are the triumph of His art;
Well may He close His eyes, but not His heart."

Herbert.

THE MASTER was on His way ascending to Jerusalem. Already fifty miles from Hermon had been traversed on this southward journey; and Capernaum, with Peter's home as the rest-house, offered a convenient halting-place. But evidently its inhabitants were animated by a very different spirit from that of the earlier days of His blessed ministry. The streets were no longer crowded by sick folk waiting for His healing touch; nor was the synagogue open to His ministry. The seeds of jealousy and suspicion which the Pharisees had sown with such lavish eagerness had produced a harvest of tares. The atmosphere was laden with the blight of mistrust. Faces were averted that used to smile.

One symptom of this changed attitude presented itself almost immediately on His arrival. The collectors of the Temple tax, which was a voluntary levy on all Jews, encountered Peter with the challenge, "Doth not your Master pay the half-shekel?" This tax was of very ancient origin, dating from the days of Moses, and supplied the funds required for the maintenance of the Temple services. It was a voluntary tax, and must therefore be distinguished from the Roman taxes, which were obligatory on Jew and Gentile alike. Religious teachers, such as Rabbis, were exempted from the payment of the Temple tax by general consent; and the universal respect which was paid our Lord in the earlier days of His ministry gave Him complete immunity from any question as to His liability to pay it. But now that He had lost caste and was being hunted down by Herod and the rulers, Peter, as His representative, was accosted with a challenge which proved that the cordon of respect and reverence which had formerly surrounded Him was broken down. There may have been a further insinuation that the Lord had veered over to the Sadducee party, who were extremely lax about the whole matter.

Peter said at once that his Master would certainly pay the tribute; but when he reached the home he learnt that Jesus knew all about the demand, for he was anticipated in his story by the question whether it was customary for kings to demand tribute from their sons. Surely the hasty promise that the tribute should be paid was incompatible with the confession of only a few days before—"the Son of the living God."

This brief conversation made it clear that our Lord had noticed the change in the treatment that He might henceforth expect; but He had no intention of standing on His rights. Since no principle was involved, He would not contest the demand. What course should be adopted must be settled not in the high court of conscience, but the lower one of expediency, and by the effect which His attitude would exert on the most conservative school of His opponents. They would be certain to catch at a refusal as a fresh ground for prejudicing Him and His teaching before the people; and a fresh stumbling-block would be cast in their path. Lest, therefore, the most scrupulous conscience should be offended, He declared that He was willing to meet the demand for them both.

A profound principle is involved here, which calls for our careful heed. When questions arise in life, *which do not involve principle and conscience*, we should be prepared to make concessions to the conscientious scruples of those whom we may be able to influence for good. In 1 Cor. ix. the Apostle Paul acted on that principle. He insisted that he was free from many things, to which he nevertheless conformed, for the sake of maintaining his influence on some whom he desired to lead afterwards into the liberty of Christ. In Christ he was free of all, but for Christ's sake he became the servant of all. All things, he said, were lawful to him, but not all things were expedient, because they failed to edify, and might prove a stumbling-block to others. "Give no occasion of stumbling, either to Jews, or to Gentiles, or to the Church of God; even as I pleased all men in all things, not seeking my own profit, but the profit of many, that they may be saved."

As Christians we dare not make payments which will conflict with conscience, but where conscience is not concerned we must be ready to meet any legitimate demand made by public use and custom. Asserting our freedom, we must not give needless offence; and in this our Lord will never fail to be our partner. He is ever willing to become surety for payments made in His Name and for the sake﹥ His Gospel.

I. CHRIST PAYS THE CHARGES FOR HIS PENNILESS DISCIPLES.— At His bidding Peter had left all to follow Him. Boats, nets, and the fish-market were forsaken. If he still kept his boat, it was only to assist his Master in His strenuous life. Months had passed since he was seen among his old fisher companions. No income, therefore, accrued from his craft for the upkeep of his home; and without doubt the Master arranged that a certain amount should be allocated from the common purse for the maintenance of that home and its in-mates. Whenever you give yourself absolutely to Christ and His service, not at your whim, but by His direct invitation, you may reckon absolutely on His thoughtful provision; and even if your faith should give out, He will remain faithful, for He cannot deny Himself.

The two women—Peter's wife and her mother—may have viewed this arrangement from the first with a certain amount of distrust, and during the absence of the whole party thirty miles to the north their faith must have been put to the test, for clearly, on Peter's arrival home, there was not a single coin left to meet this tax. They had expended their entire store; and Peter must have been startled by the glaring contrast between the glory of the Transfiguration vision, with his proposal for three tabernacles there, and the actual exigencies of his own humble home. We, who get away to our Conventions and Retreats, must never lose sight of the loving and loyal hearts that are left behind "by the stuff." It is not befitting that we should disport ourselves on the slopes of Hermon, unless we are thoughtful and careful for those whom we have left in the fisherman's home.

Peter rightly felt that this burden was not for himself to carry alone. By his summons to leave all, his Master had clearly made Himself liable for such demands. There could be no doubt as to the issue, though the precise manner of deliverance was not apparent. It was an immense relief, therefore, to find himself forestalled and anticipated before he could relate his case—Christ knew of it and was prepared with a reply.

Take heart, my friend! Before you call, He will answer, and while you are yet speaking His ready help is nigh. He knows that for His sake you have renounced many things that are legitimate for others. They have not been called to your life of consecration and self-denial. For Christ's sake you have renounced sources of income about which other Christian persons have no scruples. For the Gospel's sake you have renounced a love that, however pure in itself, refused to go all lengths for God. For the sake of dying multitudes in the far-off lands you are breaking away from old moorings and launching out into untried scenes. Be of good cheer! Your Master is not unmindful. In some way or other He will make good. Do not hesitate to take your need to Him. He cannot fail! Every one who has left houses, or brethren, or sisters, or father, or mother, or children or lands for His Name's sake shall receive a hundredfold.

With what awe Peter must have taken his disused fishing-line from the nail and gone forth on the lake, wondering where to cast his hook, but sure that through the depths some fish was being guided through "the path of the sea" towards him. According to its wont, the fish had caught at a glittering coin, dropped by a passenger or a child over a boatside. It had carried its unwelcome burden till able to disgorge it into Peter's wondering hands; and then, thrown back in the water, it had gone on its way, little weening how it had served its Creator's purpose. If not by such a miracle, yet somehow the Lord will ever meet the need of His devoted servants. None of them that trust in Him shall be desolate. He has but to open His hand, and He can satisfy the desire of them that fear Him. The tax-gatherer is ever at our door with his demand, but Jesus will be equal to every emergency.

II. OUR MASTER LINKS HIMSELF TO A SINFUL MAN.—"That take and give for Me and thee." It should be noted that the fish yielded not two half-shekels, but one coin—the stater—which was their equivalent. The conjunction *and* should be noted also, as the golden link between the Saviour and His weak and fallible disciple. This surely is the wonder of Eternity—that He should call us brethren, that He should identify Himself with us before His Father and the holy angels, that He should request that we should be with Him where He is, beholding His glory and included in His eternal Kingdom. Sometimes it seems incredible, but it was determined by the counsels of God before the first seraph broke into song, and it is verified by the experience of all the Christian centuries.

I see Him exhausted but triumphant when the forty days' temptation are concluded, when the Prince of this world has tried all lures in vain, and He smiles radiantly, promising that I too shall tread on the lion and adder. He says, "This is for Me and thee." I see Him in the garden glade, as He drains to the dregs the cup which the Father puts into His hands; His voice falters with the extremity of His grief, but He tells me that He has overcome not for Himself alone, but for me. He says again, "This is for Me and thee."

I see Him dying yonder on the Cross. The iron has entered His soul. The mid-day mid-night has just passed. He cries like a conqueror, "It is finished," and as He does so, He catches sight of me bathed in tears of anguish at its foot, and assures me that His obedience into death was necessary to fulfil the Father's will; but it is also for my redemption. He says yet a third time, "This is for Me and thee."

I see Him emerging from the tomb in the dawn of the third day. He has robbed Death of its sting and the Grave of its victory. I hear His glad announcement, "I am He that liveth and was dead, and behold I am alive for evermore"; and as He passes along the garden path He assures me that in Him I also am risen. Again He says, "This is for Me and thee."

Finally, I stand with the little group on Olivet, when He is parted from them, and a radiant chariot cloud receives Him from our sight; and as His presence fades on my mortal vision, His voice drops from above, saying, "I go to receive a Kingdom; I will ask the Father, and He shall give Me the Holy Spirit in His mighty fulness to reside for ever in My Divine human nature, and I will impart Him to thee also"; and once more He says, "This is for Me and thee."

Thus He links Himself to a sinful man, and who shall separate what God hath joined together? Neither life nor death, things present or to come, can snap that link.

III. CHRIST MAKES MORTALS HIS ALMONERS.—"Take and give for Me and thee." He has received gifts for men, and yearns to bestow them; but for this purpose He requires almoners to distribute to the crowd, as of old His Apostles took from His hands the bread and fish, and gave to the five thousand men, together with women and children. He might have addressed these same words to them: "Take and give."

Is not this the law of Christ's own life? Having received of the Father the promise of the Paraclete, He shed Him forth with both hands on the waiting Church. It pleased the Father that in Him all the fulness should dwell, and of that fulness have all we received, and grace upon grace. If we may dare put it so, our Lord has received His inheritance from the Father, and has given it all away to us, as co-heirs with Himself. He has taken and given. From the storehouse of eternity He has received the First-born share, in ingots of gold, but has changed them into common coin, that we in turn may take and give. "Being enriched in everything unto all liberality, which worketh thanksgiving to God."

The flowers are always taking from sunshine, dew, and air what they give forth in colour, fragrance, and beauty. In the carboniferous age the gigantic vegetable growths took out of the unstinting sun-power the forces that coal gives back in our hearths and furnaces. The dumb animals are ever taking from the herbage of the mountains or the grass-lands of the valleys the nutriment, which they impart to us by the sacrifice of life. Great scientists are constantly engaged in studying how to get more help from the mysterious forces which surround us. They cut cunning channels which we call machinery, and which tap the great rivers of energy as they flow through the highways of the Universe, that ordinary folk may talk through the telephone, speak down rays of light, and fill the highways with their motors. The law of all discovery is take and give.

The tragic failure of innumerable multitudes is that they have not learned to take. They pray, and pray fervently, but they have not acquired the art of taking or receiving. Our Lord said, "All things whatsoever ye pray and ask for, believe that you have *taken* them, you shall have them." And the Apostles sent to the Roman Christians this emphatic message: "The gift of God by the grace of the one man has abounded to the many . . . and they that *take* the abundance of grace shall reign in life." The Apostle does not bid us *pray* for the abundance of grace, but calls on us to *take* it. One of the great problems in the art of prayer is the delimitation of the frontiers between Importunity and Taking.

With many taking is a lost art. They pray, but fail to take. Herein is the source of bitter disappointment. We pray, agonize, and strive, but often fail to see that the cargo has already been delivered on the wharf, and is in the depôt, waiting to be claimed and fetched away. Before we can take we must be sure that we are not prompted by personal ambition, but are acting in the Name (i.e., according to the Nature) of our Lord, and are standing on the distinct warrant of a promise. When these conditions are fulfilled, we hear our Father's voice, as we stand in His holy presence, saying: "Child, thou art ever with Me, and all that I have is thine; take, and go thy way to give." We may not *feel* to have received. Ours is the reckoning of a naked faith on the unfailing faithfulness of God. We go forth to act on the assurance that we have received, that our supplies are ample and inexhaustible, that whatever demands may knock at our door, our Master will adequately meet them all.

We cannot give unless we have learned to take; and we cannot take unless we are prepared to give. If we endeavour to take with no plan or intention of giving, we shall find that our hand falls paralysed by our side. The faithless servant who received the talent, and buried it for his own use, when needed, forfeited it.

Let us go forth to give. There are aching hearts, marred lives, dumb, outstretched, open hands on all sides. Let us be channels through which God may answer prayers, and almoners, to whom He shall be able to make all grace abound, because He knows that we shall abound to every good work. He will feed the stream from inexhaustible fountains. He will minister seed for sowing, and will provide bread for the sower. His Angels shall minister to us. All our needs will be met according to His riches in glory. Give, and it shall be given to you; good measure, pressed down, shaken together, and running over, shall Christ give into your bosom, for with what measure ye mete, He will measure to you again. Wherefore "Take and give."

XI

THE SHEPHERD ON THE WATCH

MATT. xviii. 1–22; xix. 23–30; xxi. 18–22.

"Thou know'st our bitterness—our joys are Thine—
No stranger Thou to all our wanderings wild:
Nor could we bear to think, how every line
Of us, Thy darken'd likeness and defiled,
Stands in full sunshine of Thy piercing eye,
But that Thou call'st us Brethren: sweet repose
Is in that word—the Lord who dwells on high
Knows all, yet loves us better than He knows."

Keble.

IN HIS High-Priestly prayer, recorded in John xvii., our Lord, speaking specially of His Apostles, said: "While I was with them in the world, I kept them in Thy Name: those that Thou gavest me I have kept, and none of them is lost, but the son of perdition." In this allusion to His keeping we have a glimpse into the cure of souls, in which the Master was and is constantly engaged. He was no hireling. When He saw the stealthy approach of the wolf, so far from fleeing, He went before the little flock (as He called the Apostolic band) and encountered the foe. He knew that the shepherd would be smitten, and the sheep scattered; but He never desisted from warning them day and night with tears. He saw that Satan had desired to sift them as wheat and had obtained his desire, and He had specially prayed for the one whose temperament might belie him into momentary denial, but whose love He never doubted, and whose dementing agony of soul He foresaw.

We must never forget that our Lord dealt with His Apostles, not only in a group, but as individuals; not in the abstract, but the concrete; that He studied their idiosyncrasies, and administered special correction or instruction as each required. His words, therefore, as recorded by the Evangelists, had probably a special reference to encourage or repress some trait of character which He had noticed. Each of that inner circle had strong personal characteristics, which must be studied and trained, before they were prepared for the special work which awaited them, as foundation stones in the New Jerusalem. It would appear that Judas and Peter gave Him most concern. The one because his nature was so secretive and subtle, the other because his fervid and impulsive temperament was constantly hurrying him into extreme positions, from which he needed to be extricated. At one moment he would say, "Depart from me"; at the next he would leave all to follow. Now he has won the high encomium, "Blessed art thou"; and again he is addressed as Satan. In the same breath, "Thou shalt never wash my feet," and "not my feet only." Within a single hour he is ready to fight for the Master, whom he passionately loved, and denies that he had ever known Him. That such an one should ultimately be taught stability of character, enabling him to lead the Church in its conflict with a world-in-arms, presented a serious problem to his Master and Friend. He never doubted the sincerity of his affection, but was sorely tried by its fitful and impulsive exhibitions.

THE CASE OF JUDAS.—We may not linger over the Lord's watch and warning in the case of Judas, but many of His sayings must have been suggested by the change which was passing over the once-promising young man from Kerioth. He perceived with bitter sorrow that the love of money was eating out his soul, and in many of His utterances must have had him in mind. "A man's bitterest foe may arise from his own household." "No disciple of Mine should provide gold, silver, or brass in his purse for personal use." "A man's life consisteth not in the abundance of things that he possesses." "Dives lifted up his eyes, being in torments." "The unfaithful servant was cut asunder, and his portion was appointed among the unbelievers." "Ye cannot serve God and Mammon." "Comrade, stop and bethink thee, ere it is too late, to what a degree of wickedness and ingratitude thou art come." These words are applicable to us all, but they had special significance for Judas; and perhaps—speaking after the manner of men—they were elicited by the special significance of his alarming deterioration.

Similarly we may trace a personal reference to Peter's condition of soul during the latter months of our Lord's earthly ministry.

THE CASE OF PETER.—There were several particulars in regard to which he needed to be specially cautioned and strengthened:

(1) *In the Struggle for Pre-eminence.* Though Peter is not specially mentioned, we are not doing him a manifest injustice to suppose that he took a prominent part in the hot disputes which broke out from time to time, especially after our Lord's award of the keys, the reference to the significance of his name, and his inclusion with two others in that memorable Transfiguration scene. The probability of this supposition is confirmed by the fact, recorded by Mark, writing at Peter's own dictation, that when our Lord reached Capernaum, on His return from Mount Hermon, on entering "the house," which, of course, was Peter's, He asked them, "What was it that ye disputed among yourselves by the way?" At first they held their peace, for by the way they had disputed among themselves who should be the greatest. Then He sat down, and called them around Him, and said: "The only way in which a man can become first in My Kingdom is by being last of all and servant of all." Then He took a child—tradition says that it was one of Peter's own children, who afterwards became the Bishop and Martyr Ignatius—folded the happy boy in His arms, and said: "Whosoever shall receive one of such children in My Name receiveth Me."

The struggle for supremacy broke out again, when James and John endeavoured to secure a verdict in their favour by getting their mother to ask for the right-hand and left-hand places in the Kingdom. And on the eve of the Betrayal there was a recurrence of the same strife, which hindered every one of them from volunteering, in the absence of a servant, to wash the feet of the rest, though the ewer and towel, provided by the thoughtful courtesy of the host, were there ready to their hand.

Probably this ambition for the foremost place led Peter to insist that though all the others failed and forsook in the approaching hour of trail, certainly he might be counted on, "Although all shall be offended, yet will not I. Though I should die with Thee, yet will I not deny Thee." And he meant every word he spoke. We have just used the word *ambition*; but there were softening, sweetening ingredients in his strenuous affirmations. There were present, at least, a passionate devotion, a resolve that no hurt, which he could ward off, should touch that revered body, and the inner consciousness that it would be easier and far better to die with Christ than live without Him.

But if our Lord's warnings as to the peril of His Apostle were not availing, then probably nothing could so effectually have burnt out this love of pre-eminence as the denial and failure of the Betrayal night. We find no traces of the old spirit in the subsequent references to our Apostle. He takes, indeed, the foremost place in the incidents related in Acts i. and ii. without ostentation of affectation; but in the First Council of the Church, described in Acts xv., the presidency is occupied by James, whilst Peter contributes his opinion, as one amongst the rest. Finally, in his First Epistle he exhorts the elders on the ground, not of his Apostolate, but of being himself an elder and an eyewitness of the sufferings of Christ; and, surely, it is not in entire forgetfulness of his own failure that he adds: Feed the flock of God, "not as being lords over God's heritage, but as examples to the flock."

(2) *In Respect to Forgiveness.* On one occasion, when the Lord had been giving instruction on the duty of forgiveness, Peter broke in with the inquiry, "Lord, how oft shall my brother sin against me, and I forgive him?" and further suggested that seven times was the limit, which he could not be expected to exceed. Our Lord swept away the suggestion as unthinkable. It was an old Jewish notion, which must be utterly submerged in the love that He would shed abroad on the world. Calvary and Pentecost would open sluice-gates of unlimited mercy. "Jesus saith unto him, I say not unto thee, Until seven times, but until seventy times seven." Then, in the parable of the unforgiving servant, which followed, sin against a fellow-man was contrasted with the enormity of sin against God; and the Divine compassion, which releases and forgives debts of ten thousand talents, was described in glowing words, though the Divine Speaker said nothing of the cost in ransom blood which He would soon be paying in flowing streams from His own heart.

Our Lord knew, though Peter had no inkling of it, that an hour was near when His Apostle would find himself guilty of a ten-thousand-talent sin, compared with which the vilest affront ever received from a fellow-mortal would appear to be but as an hundred pence; and at such time he would cling to the hope suggested by this parable, as a drowning man to the rope thrown out for his rescue.

May we not imagine Peter hurrying through the streets, on which the grey dawn was breaking sadly, and making for the garden, where only three or four hours before he had slept whilst his Master was in agony. How could he have said those terrible words? That he had failed where he had vowed to be strong, and had added oaths and cursings which had not soiled his lips for many years! That the Master had heard all! And that look! What could he say, or whither go? Should he take his life? Remorse was choking his breath. Then there stole over his heart the words: "I say not unto thee, Until seven times, but until seventy times seven." Did my Lord expect me to do so much, and will He not do the same? And did He not say that the lord of the servant was moved with compassion, released the poor debtor at his feet, and forgave a debt of ten thousand talents? Surely He must have meant *me*! And long after he wrote: "Love as brethren, be pitiful, be courteous, not rendering evil for evil, but contrariwise blessing. . . . He bare our sins in His own body on the tree. . . . Love covereth the multitude of sins."

(3) *In the Matter of Reward.* When the young man, unable to pay the price of discipleship, had turned sorrowfully away, Peter broke in on the Saviour's disappointment with the question: "Lo! we have left all and followed Thee, what shall we have therefore?" Clearly the hope of reward was bulking largely on his vision. There would surely be a conspicuously handsome return for the sacrifices and privations that discipleship had involved, to say nothing of those to which the Master frequently alluded as imminent. But bargain-making after this fashion was clearly inadmissible in the Kingdom of Heaven, and therefore the Parable of the Labourers in the Vineyard was uttered to teach, in unforgettable imagery, that in the service of God a spirit of trust in His grace must exorcise and supersede a spirit of bargaining and barter.

The labourers had waited in the market-place from early dawn. It was through no fault of theirs that they were not on the hillside among the vines. "No man had hired them." It was not until almost sundown that they had their chance. But when, after one brief hour of service, they came to be paid, they received a whole day's pay for that brief spell. Their reward was reckoned not as of debt, but of grace. It was in happy mood that these short-time men made for their homes. Their women-folk had watched them standing in the market-place all through the day, and had made up their minds to pinch and scrape; but here was a day's wage placed in their hands. Yes! What the owner of the vineyard had been heard saying to one of the grumblers, "Is thine eye evil, because I am good," was perfectly true—he *was* good.

It was as if our Lord had said, in answer to Peter's question: "It is true that thou camest early into the vineyard. Thou wert among the first. Also, thou hast borne the burden and heat of the day, and more also is to fall to thy lot; but when thou hast completed the task, thou wilt only have done thy duty, and thy reward will be according to the riches of God's grace."

This also in coming days may have afforded the broken-hearted Apostle some comfort, as he said to himself: "It is true that I was among the first to obey the Master's summons, but I have forfeited all right to reward, even if once I cherished some hope of merit: I am not worthy to be called an Apostle; I take my place with the woman who was a sinner, and with Zaccheus the publican; but the Master said that the reward was not determined by service, but by grace. It is not of him that willeth or worketh, but of God that shows mercy. God be merciful to me the sinner, and in me first may the Master show forth all longsuffering."

(4) *In Regard to Faith.* As they passed by one morning they saw a withered fig-tree which had been cursed with barrenness on the previous day, as a warning to the Apostles and to Israel. And Peter, calling to remembrance, saith unto Jesus, "Rabbi, behold, the fig-tree which Thou cursedst is withered away." And Jesus, answering, saith unto them, "Have faith in God." A better rendering of that remarkable injunction would be, Hold on to God's Faith; or, Reckon on God's Faithfulness.

We lay stress, and rightly so, on Faith; but there are days in human life when our faith seems about to expire, like a tiny taper in a storm of wind. We cry, "Lord, I believe, help Thou my unbelief, for my unbelief is more than my belief." Our faith is as a grain of mustard seed, the least of all seeds, whilst our difficulties block our path like a mountain-range. Even the Saviour Himself feels bound to interpose a prayer lest our faith fail utterly. Then it is a source of infinite consolation to turn our thoughts away from our faith to God's Faithfulness, to hold on to it, to reckon on it, and to cry: "If we believe not, He abideth faithful; He cannot deny Himself."

In that storm-burst which broke on Peter's soul on that fateful night, with what comfort must he have stayed himself on these precious words: "Hold on to God's Faith; Reckon on God's Faithfulness; Dare to believe that He abideth Faithful and is not Unrighteous to forget." His own faith had failed, but God's Faithfulness was like the great mountains.

XII

THE EVENING OF THE DENIAL

MATT. xxvi. 17–20; MARK xiv. 12–17; LUKE xxii. 7–16;
JOHN xiii. 1–20.

"Nor lack I friends long-tried and near and dear,
Whose love is round me like this atmosphere,
Warm, soft, and golden. For such gifts to me
What shall I render, O my God, to Thee."

Whittier.

THE MOUNT of Olives, during the Passover, was covered by a large number of families, gathered from all parts of the country, and from many lands. Unable to find accommodation in the overcrowded city, they provided for themselves slight booths or tents, their cattle tethered alongside, the maidens thronging to the wells with their pitchers, whilst the children played under the shadow of the ancient olive-trees or visited the Holy City with their parents in an ecstasy of enjoyment.

It would be pleasant to think that our Lord was the guest of the dear home at Bethany, where Lazarus and his sisters loved to welcome Him; but it is more than likely that, after the Supper in the house of Simon on the evening of his arrival, He deliberately held aloof, lest His friends might become entangled in the web, which was being woven about Himself. Already the chief priests were consulting to put Lazarus to death, because by reason of him many of the Jews believed on Jesus. We have often thought, also, that if He had been her guest, Martha, the careful housewife, would never have allowed Him to leave her house in the early morning without the breakfast which, in default of her, He looked for beneath the thick foliage of a wayside tree. "The foxes have holes, the birds of the air nests, but the Son of man had not where to lay His head."

In the meanwhile the Passover was drawing nigh, and with it the treachery of Judas, the denial by Peter, and desertion on the part of them all. It is, however, with Peter's share in the happenings of the last evening of Christ's earthly life that we are now dealing. Jesus knew that the hour had come when He should depart out of this world to the Father. He knew also that He had come from God and went to God; and that the Father had given all things into His hand. With this knowledge was blended an over-brimming love. "Having loved His own which were in the world, He loved them to the end" —not only of time, but of the high-water mark of love. So we have heard the murmur of the summer-ocean, too deep for sound or foam, when it has reached to the submerging and floating of the dark lines of seaweed which lay beyond the reach of ordinary tides.

It is practically certain, therefore, that He was more concerned for "His own," and especially for Peter, than for Himself. Hence the following precautions:

I. HE PROVIDED HIM WITH A FRIEND.—The priceless worth of friendship was a matter of daily experience with the Lord. He made no secret of the tender intimacy which knit His soul with that of the disciple whom He loved, and who, more than any other, has interpreted to the world the secret workings of His heart. He realized, therefore, how much a Friend of the right kind would mean for Peter in his abandonment to the black current of a remorse which threatened despair.

Jesus could trust John utterly. The ultimate proof of His confidence was given when, from the Cross, He committed His mother to the filial care of His beloved friend. Thus He knew what John would be to Peter in the hour of black darkness, and therefore threw them together in His last sacred commission. We are expressly told that He sent Peter and John, saying, "Go and prepare us the Passover, that we may eat." Thus He set His seal on their old-time friendship.

They had been boys together, sitting side by side in the Rabbi's school, wandering in search of boyish adventure over the hills, or sharing the pleasures and perils of the fishing-fleet. Together they had grown to manhood, familiar with the hardships of the Roman occupation, with the stories passing from lip to lip of recent efforts at revolt, and with the hopes and expectations of those who were looking for the Redemption of Israel. Together they had left their homes and nets, first to give enthralled attention to the Baptist, and then to follow Jesus. Probably from the first they had been attracted to each other by an instinctive consciousness that each supplied what the other lacked. It is more than probable that each chose the other as companion when the twelve were sent out two by two.

With James, the brother of John, they had shared as partners in the miraculous draught of fishes; had stood side by side when the little daughter of Jairus awoke beneath the touch and summons of Jesus from her death-sleep. They had shared in the wonder of the Holy Mount, and had listened, on the previous night, to the Apocalyptic unveiling of the signs of the Advent and the close of the Age.

Our Lord had often noticed and rejoiced in this congenial comradeship. He knew how much it would mean for them both and for His cause when His outward presence was withdrawn. He therefore took special pains to cement and hallow it by this expression of confidence.

The result justified His fond anticipations. It was to John that Peter naturally turned, when the storm was expending its full fury on his soul. Mary of Magdala found them together on Easter morning. Together they ran to the sepulchre. Much as John loved his friend, he could not help out-running him, because of another love which had a prior claim, but he made compensation shortly afterwards by refusing to take advantage of the keener sight of his younger eyes that had discerned the Lord standing on the shore in the morning haze. In a whisper of reverent love he passed on the news to his friend, and was only glad to know, as he saw him plunge into the water and strike swiftly to the shore, that he had secured for him a moment of private fellowship and a further assurance of forgiveness from those gentle lips.

They were much together in the coming days. They went together to the Temple at the hour of prayer. Peter spoke for them both when he said to the lame man, "Look on us." They stood side by side when arrested by the Sanhedrin, and spent a memorable night together in the prison. Together they returned to their own company, and like the diverse metals of a compensating balance, they directed the policy of the infant Church. Events separated them in after years—John to Ephesus and Peter to Babylon, but that the old love remained is evident, if the slight and tender reference which

John makes to the lapse of his friend is contrasted with the explicit and circumstantial account which Peter gives in the Second Gospel. It is not good that man should be alone, especially in hours when he remembers his sins, and is distracted with the inner warfare. The Lord anticipates such need, and before it arises provides a Jonathan for David, a John for Peter, a Timothy for Paul, a Melanchthon for Luther, a Burns for Hudson Taylor, and a Faithful or Hopeful for Christian.

II. He assured him of a Complete Cleansing.—"Clean every whit." Not improbably Judas had planned to capture the whole party at the Paschal Feast, his plan was, however, anticipated and defeated by Christ's arrangement—probably made beforehand with some secret disciple—that the meeting-place should only be known to the Apostles when they reached the city. The traitor was therefore compelled to postpone the final scene till nightfall, being certain that the Master would spend that night, as previously, in the garden. "Judas, also, who betrayed Him, knew the place, for Jesus ofttimes resorted thither with His disciples." But in the meanwhile there was security for one brief hour of holy fellowship and farewell, the more especially when the traitor had withdrawn.

With desire He had desired to eat that Supper with the chosen band before He suffered. It would be for His own comfort and strength, and for theirs. He therefore committed the necessary preparations to His two devoted friends, sure that no detail would be omitted which their love or forethought could anticipate. Deeply impressed with the increasing gravity of the position, they secured the lamb, brought it early to the priest for killing, purchased the bitter herbs, Passover-cakes, and skin of wine, and hastened back to prepare the humble repast. It was all that their means permitted, for Judas held the bag, and appropriated a large proportion of its contents.

The city was too preoccupied and crowded to notice the famous Teacher and His companions as they passed through the Kedron-gate and made for the appointed meeting-place. The sky was already darkening, and the earlier stars were beginning to appear. Apparently the embers of jealous rivalry were still smouldering, and burst into a flame as soon as the large upper room, where Peter and

John had been at work all the afternoon, was reached. The walk had been hot and dusty, and all would have been thankful for the customary ablutions, common to every Jewish home. In this case, however, they were wanting. Ewer, basin, and towel were provided, but no servant could be spared from the household at that busy season. Would no Apostle perform this office for the rest, and specially for the Lord? Apparently none volunteered. To undertake menial duty would, in their judgment, be equivalent to signing a deed of abdication from the throne of power, which each was claiming. There was also the question of precedence at the table to be considered. Even if the couch on the Lord's right hand were conceded to John, who should be on His left? Ought not Peter, to whom all were indebted for his efforts to prepare the feast? But Judas insisted as treasurer, on his superior claims. The atmosphere was charged with feverish passion, and the peaceful enjoyment of the feast, on which Jesus had set such store, was seriously threatened. To arrest further discussion the Lord arose from the supper table, laid aside His outer garments, girded Himself with the towel, as any household servant might have done, poured water into the basin, and began to wash His disciples' feet, wiping them carefully with the towel.

A sudden silence must have befallen, as He passed from one to another in this lowly ministry, until He came to Peter, who had been watching the process with shame and indignation. "Dost Thou wash my feet?" he exclaimed; "my feet shall never be washed by Thee." How little he realized that a still more drastic cleansing must soon be administered by those gentle hands, or he could have no part with Jesus in the world-mission of Redemption! "If I wash thee not, thou hast no part with Me!" Evidently Peter caught his Master's meaning. The outward was symbolic of the inward, the physical of the spiritual; and he replied: "Lord, not my feet only, but also my hands and my head."

It was as though he requested that his soul-life might there and then receive a fresh beginning, and that his entire being might be replunged into the fountain opened for sin and uncleanness. "Make sure work this time, my Lord, let me begin again, as I began at the first, with Thee in my boat!"

"No," said Jesus in effect, "that is not necessary. He who has recently bathed does not require entire immersion, if hands or feet are befouled. It is sufficient for the soiled member to be cleansed, and the body is every whit clean. When My disciples fall into sin, there is no necessity for them to commence their religious life afresh. It is enough if the particular sin, of which they are aware, is confessed and put away. Whenever that confession is made and that cleansing sought, I will show Myself faithful and just to forgive the sin and cleanse from all unrighteousness."

There was therefore a double significance in our Lord's lowly act of feet-washing. He taught the royalty of service, and also that sin does not sever the regenerate soul from God. If we are overtaken with a fault, it is not required that we go back again to the wicket-gate, but that we should be restored and led back to the narrow path. The disciple is still a disciple; the child still a child. There must be confession, and there will be instant restoration. "Restore such an one in the spirit of meekness, considering thyself, lest thou also be tempted."

Peter must have been greatly comforted by this incident, when he lay under the shadow of his great sin. He was not a castaway. He had not forfeited his part in the Book of Life or in the Holy City. There was no need for him to begin from the beginning. The Lord would wash his soiled feet, and he would be clean every whit. God's work in his soul had received a set-back, but it had not ceased. He need not enter a second time by the door of the New Birth; but he must turn again, and from his failure learn to strengthen his brethren. There was a world of difference between the apostasy of Judas and the backsliding of Peter!

What a wealth of comfort has been ministered by this lowly act of the Saviour to those whose feet have become soiled by the dust of earth's highways! He knew that He had come from God, was going to God, and was God; but to wash the feet of these simple men did not seem incongruous with the throne to which He went. And now that He, as the Lamb slain, is on the throne, He will turn aside from the adoration of eternity, and "stay His ear for every sigh a contrite suppliant brings."

XIII

"LET NOT YOUR HEART BE TROUBLED"

MATT. xxvi. 21–25, 31–35; LUKE xx, 21–23;
JOHN xiii. 21–38, xiv. 1, 2.

"Heart, heart, awake! The love that loveth all
Maketh a deeper calm than Horeb's cave:—
God in thee—can His children's folly gall?
Love may be hurt, but shall not love be brave?"
Macdonald.

ON THE appearance of the first three stars, a blast from the silver trumpets of the Temple gave the signal for the Passover-supper to begin in all parts of the city. On the table were the bread, wine, water and herbs; on the side-table the roasted lamb. The swinging lamps were aglow above, and below, around the table, were the thirteen couches. Everything bespoke the preparation of the two Apostles. For hundreds of years the same customs had been followed, the same explanations given, the same psalms sung, the same blessings and thanksgivings pronounced. But the Apostles were conscious that a heavy cloud was upon the Master's soul, to which He presently gave the clue when He said: "Verily I say unto you, that one of you shall betray Me." And again: "One of you that eateth with Me shall betray Me." And yet again: "It is one of you who dippeth his hand with Me in the dish. . . . It were better for him that he had never been born."

Each disciple, except Judas, seems to have suspected himself more than any of his fellows, and said distrustfully: "Master, is it I?" But Peter, impatient of the uncertainty, and perhaps anxious to be sure that he at least was not intended, made a secret sign to John to ascertain to whom the Lord referred. In a whisper, as he leant back on the Saviour's bosom, John asked who the traitor would be. Jesus did not wish to utter his name, and replied, again in an undertone, which probably only Peter, John, and Judas caught: "It is he to

89

whom I shall give the sop when I have dipped it." Then placing some
bitter herbs between slices of bread, He dipped the morsel into a
special bowl of mixed fruits called "Charosheth," and passed it to
Judas. The traitor then knew that the Master knew; but with brazen
effrontery, he said: "Master, is it I?" Under His breath our Lord
replied: "It is as thou hast said"; and then louder, so that every one
around the table heard Him, "That thou doest, do quickly."

The traitor could no longer bear the white light of Christ's holy
presence. Perhaps remorse had already begun to gnaw at his vitals.
Hastily wrapping his cloak around him, he went out into the night;
but the revealing words had been spoken so gently that only Peter
and John were in the secret. Even they did not suppose that matters
had gone so far, and that the thirty pieces of silver—"the price of
blood"—were already in Judas's purse. So well had he played his
part, that the rest supposed that the Lord had commissioned him to
buy some additional article for the feast, or that he had gone out to
make some offering to the poor.

His absence was a great relief to Jesus. What He must have
suffered for all those later months from the presence of Judas,
amongst his intimates, can only be appreciated by such as can say
with the Psalmist: "Woe is me that I sojourn in Mesech, and dwell in
the tents of Kedar! My soul hath long dwelt with him that hateth
peace." "Therefore, when he was gone out, Jesus said. . . ." And
He poured forth a volume of golden speech for the warning and
comfort of the immediate circle of "His own," and through them
of the Universal Church. We must specially concentrate on the
words addressed to Peter:

I. "LET NOT YOUR HEART BE TROUBLED!" "I HAVE PRAYED FOR
THEE."—In after years Peter compared the Tempter to a lion, roaring
around the fold, and seeking an unguarded opening or a stray sheep.
As he wrote the words, he must have had in mind the Master's warning to them all, and especially himself: "Simon, Simon, Satan hath
sought and obtained permission that he may sift all of you as wheat,
but I have prayed for thee, that thy faith may not fail in the ordeal."

There is no fear for the wheat, when the husbandman, in Oriental
fashion, throws up the grain which he has threshed against the evening breeze. Its weight brings it back to the floor, and only the chaff

disappears. It is a distinct advantage to be rid of the encumbering chaff, as it is for the Church to be freed from the presence of those who are not truly one with it. When persecution arises because of the Word, and many are offended, when iniquity abounds and the love of many waxes cold, when a controversy arises like that led by Athanasius on the behalf of evangelical truth, there is no reasonable ground for regret. It was good for Arius to leave the Church in the fourth century and Judas in the first.

It seems more than probable that the professing Church of to-day is on the edge of one of the greatest hours of purgation that has ever been experienced. The tempest will roar through the forests, snapping off all boughs not vitally connected with the trunk. A fire will be lit which only the gold, silver, and precious stones can outlast. To use the words of the Baptist: "His fan is in His hand, and He will thoroughly purge His floor." But do not fear for the *wheat*!

As a matter of fact, none of the Apostles were lost save Judas. They were proved to be wheat. Though they forsook the Master at first, they were all assembled in the Upper-room on the Resurrection-night, although the doors were shut for fear of the Jews. They all gathered around the Master on the Mount of Ascension. It is said that each, excepting John, went to Heaven in a martyr's chariot of fire. And the name of each is inscribed on the Foundations of the Holy City, the Bride of the Lamb.

In the meanwhile the Saviour's phrasing is full of comfort. Satan has to obtain permission before he sifts, and there is a limit beyond which he may not go. "God is faithful," says the Apostle, "who will not suffer you to be tempted above that ye are able." Before the enemy could touch Job's property or flesh, he must needs ask and obtain permission, and in each case a limit was imposed beyond which he might not go. It would almost seem as though a facsimile of Zachariah's vision of the desperate condition of the Priesthood, with Satan standing to resist, were presented to our Saviour's vision, and that He, as Intercessor and Friend, interposed with the remonstrance: "The Lord, who hath chosen these, rebuke thee; they shall be as brands plucked from the burning."

The virulent hatred of wicked spirits that infest the Heavenlies—i.e., the regions of spiritual existence—is a heavy addition to the difficulties which we are called to encounter in our earthly pilgrimage and warfare. The fight with Apollyon in the Valley of the Shadow of Death is a fearsome but inevitable experience. Hosts of unclean and evil spirits hover around our path awaiting the favourable moment for inveigling us to sin. They hate us because evil necessarily hates goodness, and because in our failure they can cause grief and loss to the Captain of our Salvation. But greater is He that is for us than all that be against us, and the Great High Priest, who is pledged to present us before the Father's Presence with exceeding joy, is on the watch, measuring the fiery ordeal to our strength and praying that our faith may not fail. Is it not well that we have been tempted? Temptation reveals our own weakness and drives us in penitence and faith to Christ. It reveals aspects of His saving help of which otherwise we should be ignorant. We cannot help being tempted. There is no sin in being attacked by the Evil One. Our Lord Himself suffered being tempted. We cannot but be aware of a lower nature, to which the tempter addresses himself, and which is very sensitive to his appeals. But we can resist steadfast in the faith. We can reckon that we are dead in Christ to the rule and behests of the god of this world. We can appropriate the opposite grace in Christ, so that we actually gain in the hour of trial and become more than conquerors. From every battlefield we carry off the spoil; and all through the conflict we are conscious of our Saviour's intercessions. "Thanks be unto God which giveth the Victory through Jesus Christ our Lord!"

II. "LET NOT YOUR HEARTS BE TROUBLED!" "I GO TO PREPARE A PLACE."—The unfortunate division of chapters in A.V. has hindered the full appreciation of Christ's special reference in the memorable words with which John xiv. opens. We love them, learn them, repeat them beside the dying, and write them on our memorials; but we fail to connect them with the words immediately preceding: "Peter said unto Him, Lord, why cannot I follow Thee now? I will lay down my life for Thy sake. Jesus answered him, Wilt thou lay down thy life for My sake? Verily, verily, I say unto thee, The cock shall not crow till thou hast denied Me thrice." *Then* He said, "Let not your heart be troubled. . . . In my Father's House are many mansions. . . . I go to prepare a place for you."

Our Lord's ideal of the Father's House is briefly summarized in the Parable of the Two Sons. Its principal windows look earthwards. It is the place where broken lives are received to be remade and refitted. There love is undisguised and prodigal in its welcome, and life becomes rhythmic to the music of eternity, and joy has no bounds. They that live there are ever face to face with God, and all that He has is theirs. Only there are no elder brothers to stand without; and even the menial servants rejoice with the sons and daughters as they are gathered home, one by one.

There also are "many mansions," which suggest not only spaciousness, but room for each character and individual to develop on its own particular lines. The Apostles, when following our Lord, were overshadowed by the Boanerges; there was the constant fret of overcrowding, and the possibilities for self-realization were few. But there each of the redeemed shall be able to attain to a full development. This is apparently taught us in the comparison of the Apostles to the twelve precious stones of Rev. xxi., each of which is distinct from all the rest, and each a necessary part of the foundations of the New Jerusalem. As the gardener "beds out" the crowded plants of his hothouse, so will the saints have room to be themselves, and each will have love enough, joy enough, space enough, opportunity enough, together with his own share of the Fullness and Service of Christ. Peter will still be Peter, and John John. Each star will differ from all the rest. There will be many mansions, and no need to scramble or contend for room.

But they require preparing, as Peter and John were sent to prepare for the Master's coming, with the rest. The same Greek word is employed in each case. "Master, where shall we *prepare* the Passover?"—"I go to *prepare* a place for you." Our Lord desired to eat *that* Passover, but how much more to eat as in Mark xiv. 25? In the meanwhile He is as busy in preparing as Peter and John were all that afternoon. As they thought for Him, so He is thinking for us. No Angel could do for us what He can, because He has lived amongst us in our homes, and knows exactly what makes Home. Peter on the Holy Mount proposed three slight booths, but that is an everlasting habitation. As they prepared the sacrificial lamb, in memory of the Passover in Egypt, there will be yonder in the midst of the Throne a Lamb as it had been slain. He will once more drink of the new wine of the Feast, once more gird himself and come forth to serve, once more join in singing Psalms of Rejoicing, like the great Hallel which always mingled with and closed the Feast.

But the significance of our Lord's Promise is clearly defined when we remember that He had predicted, only a few minutes before, that one should deny and all forsake. "I go to prepare a place for you"— for thee, my beloved John; for thee, Peter, when the memory of thy denial shall be as waters that pass away; for thee, Thomas, though given to doubt and pessimism; for thee, Philip, longing to be shown the Father. Not one of you shall be overlooked, not one shall miss his share. "Let not your heart be troubled, neither let it be afraid." Surely *we* may take courage, if only we are trusting Him for His justifying grace. In spite of our sins and failures, our sorrows and temptations, He will bring us through. Whom He called, them He also justified : and whom He justified, them He also glorified. "What shall we then say to these things? If God be for us, who can be against us?" "I know whom I have believed!"

III. "LET NOT YOUR HEART BE TROUBLED!" "I WILL RECEIVE YOU TO MYSELF."—Again the idea of the afternoon is repeated. When the two Apostles had finished their preparations, they went to the city-gate, or the end of the street, or at least to the doorstep, to *receive* their expected guests. In this sense our Lord's words must be understood, and they are confirmed by the fact that the martyr Stephen saw the Son of Man *standing* at the right hand of God, as though He had risen up to receive and welcome him.

It was as though the Master particularized each as He spoke: "*James*! thou wilt be the first of the noble army of martyrs. Herod will slay thee with the sword, but thou shalt have a royal reception. *Thomas*! thou wilt be sawn asunder, but I will receive thee, and an abundant entrance will be given. *John*! thou wilt linger on till all of thy generation shall have passed away, but I will be waiting for thee, and thou shalt see again the dear faces which thou hast loved and lost awhile. *Peter*! thou shalt stretch forth thine hands and be borne to a cross, but as My Father will receive My Spirit into His hands, so My hands shall receive thine. Each of you will find Me waiting for him on the doorstep of the Father's House."

"You are too dear for Me to allow you to be misled by false illusions. If Immortality and Eternal Life had been a mirage of the desert or a fond dream of the poet, I would have put you on your guard against being deceived. You believe that you are sons of God, that you shall enter into His Presence, that you shall sit down with Abraham, Isaac, and Jacob—continue to believe. If it were not so, I would have told you. Let not your heart be troubled, neither let it be afraid!"

XIV

. . . "AND PETER"

MATT. xxviii. 1–8; MARK xvi. 1–8; LUKE xxiv. 1–8; JOHN xx. 1–10.

"The storm is o'er—and hark! a still small voice
Steals on the ear, to say, Jehovah's choice
Is ever with the soft, meek, tender soul:
By soft, meek, tender ways He loves to draw
The sinner, startled by his ways of awe:
Here is our Lord, and not where thunders roll."

Keble.

AN ANCIENT tradition closely associates Peter with the authorship of the Second Gospel, which, whilst bearing the name of Mark, was probably written beneath the prompting and supervision of the Apostle. There are not a few internal corroborations of this view, both in the omissions and additions of the narrative as compared with that of Matthew or Luke. Graphic touches also abound which were clearly reminiscences of one who had been an eye witness of that wondrous life. In the forefront of these, these two words may be cited. Matthew records the angel's words to the women thus: "Go quickly and tell His disciples," but Mark makes the significant addition, *"and Peter."* With the others, those words might be obliterated by tides of time and change, but they were engraven on the rock of Peter's character and inlet with gold.

In the Song of Solomon three traits are assigned to a perfect love, and each of these was notably present in our Lord's remarkable treatment of His Apostle and friend, who had been warned thrice, had denied Him thrice, and on three different occasions was restored.

I. LOVE IS STRONG AS DEATH.—Much had happened to our Lord since that hour in the Judgment Hall when He turned and looked

96

upon Peter. He had drained to the dregs the cup which the Father gave Him to drink, in pursuance of an agreement into which they had entered before time-cycles commenced to revolve.

At His own request He had been made sin for man, that God might be just and the justifier of them who believed.

He had put away sin by the sacrifice of Himself amid rending rocks and sack-clothed skies, and the hidden face of the Father's love.

He had bowed His head in death, laying down His life of Himself, and by death had destroyed him that had the power of death.

He had met the prince of this world in the very stronghold of his power, and had wrested from his grasp the keys of Hades and of death.

He had passed through the mysterious regions of Hades, referred to afterwards as "the lower parts of the earth," and had proclaimed His finished work to the spirits, which aforetime were disobedient.

He had issued from His grave, leading captivity captive, and robbing death of its sting and the grave of its victory.

The tidings were already speeding to the farthest limits of the Universe, that through the blood of His Cross, the very heavens had been brought into closer relationship with God. Even the minstrelsy of the eternal world must have been arrested as angels desired to penetrate to the heart of the crowding revelations of that hour.

But His love was unimpaired. There was no change in its tenacity or direction. His delights were still with the sons of men. Neither death nor the grave had made any change in it; any more than they can change the love of those whom we have loved and lost awhile. Peter's case had been on His heart when He closed His eyes in death, and it was present to Him when He stopped for a moment to speak with the angel sentinel, whom He charged with this message.

To quote again the words of the Canticle—He had set Peter as a seal on His heart, the seat of love, and on His arm, the seat of power. He had carried that seal unbroken through the crowding incidents which achieved the redemption of our race; and the first words of the risen Saviour proved that His love is strong as death. Having loved His own, who were in the world, He loved them to the end. His love is *strong*. In others it may be merely emotional and affectional, expressing itself in smiles, or tears, or tendernesses, and largely composed of sentiment; but Christ's love is strong as well as tender. He is Immortal Love, but He is the Strong Son of God.

What death and the grave could not do, the lapse of Time and the glories of Heaven have not done. He loves us still, as He loved Peter and Mary, John and Thomas, in the days of His flesh. Still, He breaks the silence, uttering our names, understanding our failures, and calling us back from the far country into which we have wandered. Appropriating but reversing Peter's words, He seems to say: "Though all men should be offended because of thee, yet will I never be offended."

II. MANY WATERS CANNOT QUENCH LOVE.—Like Greek fire, Christ's love burns under water; for surely in this case, as in myriads of others, it was beset by floods of ingratitude, indifference, waywardness, denial, and sin.

Peter had failed Him in the Garden, but He sent for him.—Descending from the Upper Room to the street by the outer staircase, over which vine-leaves may have fluttered in the moonlight, Jesus led His disciples across the Kedron, and up the lower slopes of Olivet, till they reached the upland lawns, studded by olive-trees and the tents of the pilgrims. An enclosure there had apparently been placed at His disposal by the owner, to which He frequently resorted. His disciples had ofttimes entered its precincts in His company, and were somewhat startled, when He bade eight of them await His coming at the entrance, whilst three only were invited to advance farther along the grassy path, chequered by alternate moonlight and shadow. Even they were presently stayed and urged to unite in watching and prayer, whilst He went to the distance of a stone-cast. He must tread the wine-press alone, and of the people none might be with Him. Not even the beloved John could be there when He took the cup from His Father's hand.

"Watch with me," He said, as He left them. The request was prompted by his humanity, for who does not know the priceless value of sympathy in the supreme hours of life? It is easier to make springs in the valley of Baca, if we are surrounded by a pilgrim-band. Guinevere, the Queen, was comforted by the prattlings of the little maid at Glastonbury. Forasmuch as the children are partakers of flesh and blood, Jesus Himself likewise took part in the same. But

He knew also that it was the hour of the Power of Darkness. The winnowing was about to begin. Already Judas was mustering his bands. Only as they were encased in the whole armour of God could the disciples continue to stand in that evil day. But as He came three times to see how they fared, they failed Him. Their eyes were heavy with sleep; and, finally, an Angel had to furnish the strengthening which man might have rendered, but failed. Could Peter ever forget the pathos of the Master's remonstrance which was addressed specially to himself—"What, could ye not watch with me one hour?" But though Peter had failed Him, notwithstanding all his protestations, Jesus sent for him.

Peter misconceived of His Spirit and Plan and greatly endangered Him.—All the Apostles misread the situation. They had no doubt that Jesus was the Son of the Highest and the King of Israel. To the last they wrangled for the highest positions in the Kingdom. They were not altogether surprised at the approach of the armed band, which, indeed, Jesus had taught them to expect. They had even provided against such an emergency by procuring two swords, of which Peter had one. It had probably been arranged that if the need arose, they should die around His person, though they did not expect that this would be necessary. At the supreme moment God would surely interpose, Angel hosts would appear on the scene, and their foes would be scattered as in the day of Midian.

Though Peter quailed before the servantmaid, he was not cravenhearted. He would have fought like a lion, if the Lord had permitted it. The others, when they realized the situation, asked the Master to give the signal for smiting with the sword; and Peter, not waiting for the Master's word, was already in the midst of the band hacking and hewing. He struck a mighty blow on the helmet of Malchus, which glanced aside and severed his right ear. It was well meant, but it could not be permitted. The use of force would provoke retaliation. They that took the sword would perish by the sword. The dignity of the Saviour's voluntary surrender would be impaired, and His deliberate acceptance of the Cross would be beclouded. The Pharisees would be only too glad to construe their resistance as the beginning of a revolt against the Roman occupation.

Jesus had repeatedly insisted that no one took His life from Him, but that He laid it down of Himself. By the express commandment of the Father, He could surrender and resume it. But the voluntary element in His suffering would be lost sight of if He were led off after an unseemly struggle. He therefore interposed to quell the rising excitement, held back His followers, asked permission for the freeing of one hand that He might reach as far as the wounded man, and after a brief remonstrance allowed them to lead Him away as a lamb to the slaughter. This prompt action saved the situation, which Peter's impulsive act had created. But the energy of his interposition proved the more absolutely how entirely Peter and the rest had misconceived of the whole situation. But notwithstanding all, and with the knowledge that his misconceptions were still clinging to him, Jesus mentioned Peter specially, and sent this special summons for him to come.

Peter had falsified his Vows and denied Him thrice with Oaths—but He sent for him.—The band—their captive in the midst—turned back to the city. John first recovered from the panic-stricken flight, which had carried all the Apostles from their Master's side, and seems to have followed closely in the rear, whilst Peter followed afar off. On the opening of the great gates of Annas's palace, where the first informal trial for extracting further evidence was held, John entered with the crowd; but not discovering Peter, and sure that he was waiting outside, he went back and spoke to the maid, who kept the wicket-gate, on his friend's behalf. She recognized him as an acquaintance of the High Priest, and admitted Peter, scanning his features as he passed under the oil-lamp, which lighted up the porch.

This porch led to a quadrangle, open to the sky; and as the night was cold, the servants kindled a fire in the big brazier, which shed its flickering rays on the faces of the motley group that had shared in the night's adventure. Roman soldiers and Hebrew police, the servants of the High Priest and the spies and informers that were waiting to give evidence, stood and warmed themselves. John had gone "with Jesus" into the Council Chamber, the windows of which looked out on the quadrangle; but Peter joined the group around the fire. "He stood and warmed himself." He had lost heart and hope. That his Master had so evidently refused his help had disconcerted him, and perhaps had created a veil of misunderstanding and disappointment. Still he wanted to see the end, and he thought to evade discovery by joining with the rest, as though one of themselves.

The portress, who had admitted him, leaving her post, came up to the fire, recognized Peter, and rallied him before the entire circle with the challenge: "This man also was with the Galilean." He was taken unawares, but parried the attack by professing that he did not understand what she meant—"I neither know nor understand what thou sayest."

Seizing a favourable opportunity, when probably their attention was drawn in another direction, he withdrew towards the porch, and as he reached it a cock crew in the grey dawn. Whilst there he was recognized by another maid, who had probably heard the words of her fellow-servant at the fire. She remarked to a group of bystanders: "This man also was with Jesus the Nazarene." Again he denied, and this time with an oath—"I know not the man." At the expiration of an hour he was back again at the fire, perhaps with the intention, made in his own strength, of retrieving the situation. He would vindicate his Master, even though he did not identify himself with His cause! But when he opened his mouth, his inability as a Galilean to pronounce the Hebrew gutturals gave the lie to his repeated and emphatic disavowals of any attachment to Jesus. One and another denounced him; his brogue betrayed him; and the kinsman of Malchus recognized his relative's assailant. The situation was extremely threatening, and the hapless disciple began to curse and to swear, saying, "I know not this man of whom ye speak." But the more boisterous his speech, the stronger the evidence against himself.

A second time, while he was yet speaking, a cock crew, and Peter remembered the words that Jesus had spoken. Jesus also had heard, for the second time, the same sound, and had heard Peter's strident voice where He was standing. Then, forgetting His own griefs, He turned and looked at Peter, not with anger or reproach, but remembering and reminding. And yet He sent for him. Many waters cannot drown His love! We too may fail Him, deny, and crucify Him afresh. But when our heart turns back in an agony of grief and remorse, He will renew us again unto repentance. "Only so look on us, when we fail Thee, blessed Lord, that we too may be recalled from our relapse, and broken-hearted may be forgiven and restored!"

XV

"HE WAS SEEN OF PETER"

LUKE xxiv. 13–35; 1 COR. xv. 5.

" When brooding o'er remembered sin
The heart dies down—O mightest then
Come ever true, come ever near,
And wake the slumbering love again,
Spirit of God's most holy fear."
Keble.

ONLY THEY who have suffered keen remorse, as they recall some real or fancied lapse from the ideals of human love for those who have crossed the River, will appreciate the anguish with which Peter fled from the hateful scene of his denial. That last look of tender, pitying love haunted him! Could it be the last time that he should see that beloved face, or hear that familiar voice? Would he never be able to tell out his anguish and receive the assurance of forgiveness? Was this the end? Could he ever be happy again? Even if God forgave him, could he forgive himself? How could he have been entrapped in so false a deed? Why had he not kept away from the fire, or definitely left the scene when first he was recognized?

Tradition says that whenever, in coming years, he heard a cock crow, he was accustomed to fall on his knees and weep; and that he was accustomed daily to awaken at cock-crow and spend in prayer the fateful hour in which he failed his Lord. Probably neither of these is a correct version of the subsequent expression of his repentance. It is more likely that his old strong, boastful spirit received its death-wound, that he became very pitiful and tender toward the fallen, and that he came to believe, as never before, in the love of the Saviour, the coals of which gave so vehement a heat as to melt his heart into a fountain of tears. IT WAS A VERY FLAME OF JEHOVAH.

I. THE SCENE OF HIS BITTER SORROW IS NOT REVEALED.—Where did he go when he left the Palace of Annas? Surely to the Garden, that he might lie full length on the very spot of his Master's agony, and wet with his tears the sward which had been bedewed by the sweat of blood. And when the sun was up, and Jerusalem began to stir, he would make his way to the house of John, where he knew that he would be secreted even from the prying eyes of the others, who were bewildered with the events that had so suddenly swept their Master from their midst, and with Him all their hopes for this world and the next. At least they had this to be thankful for, that even if they had forsaken their Lord, yet they had not denied Him.

The morning hours passed slowly forward. He could hear that the city was moved. But probably only snatches of information floated through the open window. Now *Crucify* from ten thousand throats, and then the strange word *Barabbas*. John was too engrossed with all that was happening to return, and no other could have guessed that he was there.

Presently, about noon, there were heavy steps in the doorway, and on going to see he found John supporting, almost carrying, Mary, the Mother. In her agonized face, and in John's, he learnt that the worst had happened, and probably forbore to question them. Maybe neither of them knew at that time that he was carrying a heavier load than they.

From his first Epistle we learn that Peter was an eyewitness of the sufferings of Christ. If, as is probable, that phrase includes the sufferings of the Cross, he may have stolen through the streets over which the midday gloom was beginning to gather, that he might, even from a distance and obscurely, see the outlines of the Cross, which bore the One whom he loved with all the passion of a strong and penitent heart. He might not tarry, however, for John probably awaited his return to care for Mary, whilst he went back to stand so near the Cross as to hear the last dying cry which announced a finished Redemption and the committal of the Redeemer's Spirit to the Father.

With these details and others he returned home; and in the weary waiting-time of the following hours Peter confided all the tragic story of his fall. Happy are they who under such circumstances have such a friend. Happy also are they who, remembering their own failures and weakness, are skilful enough to bind up broken hearts. "If a man be overtaken in any trespass, ye which are spiritual restore such an one in a spirit of meekness, looking unto thyself, lest thou also be tempted. Bear ye one another's burdens, and so fulfil the law of Christ."

II.—THE FACT OF THE RESURRECTION BROKE ON HIM GRADUALLY.

—Had the whole wonder and glory broken on the Apostles suddenly, it would have overwhelmed and dazed them. It was, therefore, wisely ordered that it should be tempered, and made "by divers portions and in divers manners."

(1) *The Tomb was Empty.*—Early on Easter morning Mary of Magdala, breathless with haste, broke in on the sleepless anguish of John's home with her hastily-formed impression that the body had been taken from its resting-place by unknown hands. "They have taken away the Lord out of the tomb, and we—women who visited the spot further to embalm His body—know not where they have laid Him."

Instantly Peter was on his feet and hurried forth, followed by John, and they made for the Garden at the top of their speed. On reaching the tomb first, because younger and fleeter of foot, John contented himself with looking in. Sacred awe, reverence, wonder, and respect for ceremonial custom withheld him. But Peter, regardless of all restraint, true to his impulsive nature, could brook no delay, but went straightway into the chamber whence his Master had gone forth an hour or two before. Clearly it had not been rifled either by friend or foe. The careful disposition of the clothes made that hypothesis impossible. They had fallen together so naturally as though the body which had lain within their folds had been withdrawn without removing them, and the head-cloth was carefully folded up, as only deliberate hands would fold it. John was so impressed with what he saw that he almost guessed the truth; and Peter became thoughtful and wondering. But they needed further confirmation, for they knew not the Scripture that He must rise again from the dead; and so they went away again to their own home.

(2) *The Lord appeared to Mary Magdalene.*—This was the next stage in the unveiling of the great wonder of the Lord's Resurrection;

and evidently it made a profound impression on Peter, for it is in Mark's Gospel that we are told that when Jesus was risen early on the first day of the week He appeared first to Mary Magdalene, "from whom He had cast out seven demons." That last clause probably reveals the secret of the comfort which Christ's interview with Mary brought to his distraught soul. He well knew the story of her past, from which the Master had delivered her; and he reasoned that if Jesus had revealed Himself to *her*, had spoken *her* name in the old tone of voice, and had commissioned *her* to go to his brethren with the message of Resurrection and Ascension, there was good reason to believe that in his own case also, though all unworthy, the Lord would resume His old intimacy and comradeship.

Mary had led him to visit the empty tomb, and now, as she came a second time to the house, with the further tidings of her own experiences with Him, whom she took to be the gardener—a surmise which was more accurate than she supposed—Peter's hope took a great leap forward. To adopt his own words in after-years, he was "begotten again unto a living hope," and he was prepared for the yet more personal invitation, which was even then upon its way. The tenderness of that message could be relished with a more delicate appreciation, because it was not the first intimation of the mighty event which had just transpired.

(3) *The Message of the Women.*—They had departed quickly from the sepulchre, and ran to bring His disciples word; but they were arrested by the appearance of their Lord, who met them saying, "All hail!" They took hold of His feet and worshipped Him, and He repeated the Angel's bidding, saying, "Fear not, go tell My brethren." All this delayed them. It would appear also that, whereas Mary had gone to John and Peter, these women probably made for the other eight Apostles, who were gathered in the Upper Room; and as the Magdalene evidently hastened from the two Apostles to the eight, so the women hastened from the eight to the two, who were discussing the events of the morning, and even the Mother had staid her tears to listen with wondering expectancy.

The women broke in on them like a ray of the sun through a cloud-drift in a murky sky. They had seen the Lord! He had spoken to them! He had commissioned them to bring them glad tidings of great joy! But before they met Him, the Angel had bidden them inform His brethren *and Peter* that He was risen, and was preceding them into Galilee, where they should see Him. The women had no idea of the relevancy of those words. They looked on Peter as foremost among the disciples, and it seemed quite fitting that he should be specialized by the Angel's message; but to Peter the mention of his name was as life from the dead. Did he not start up when he heard the women mention it? Did he not question them severely, to be quite sure that the utterance of his name was not an invention of their own? Did he not insist on their recalling and repeating the whole wonderful story, with every detail of light and shade? And when they had passed on to tell "the rest," did he not quietly adore the love that would not let him go, the love that bore all things, believed all things, hoped all things, endured all things, and that never failed, until it had found and brought back the sheep that had gone astray?

III. FINALLY THE LORD APPEARED TO HIM.—In his enumeration of the witnesses of our Lord's Resurrection in 1 Cor. xv. Paul records that "He was seen of Cephas"; and when Cleopas and his friend entered the Upper Room on Easter Eve they were saluted by a chorus of glad voices, saying: "The Lord is risen indeed, and hath appeared unto Simon." That is all we know. Where they met, and when, and what passed between them—all these are hidden in Christ's heart and Peter's. Probably they will never be disclosed, even when the sea gives up its dead. Nor do we wish them to be disclosed, because we also have secrets with Christ, which we have committed to His safe keeping, with the absolute assurance that they shall never be divulged, even in that world where they know even as they are known.

What passed in that interview is not recorded, but from our own experience we can fill in the blank page. We know that there must have been bitter tears, broken words, long breaks of silence when speech was over-borne, assurances that the penitent did really love, whatever might be argued to the contrary from word or act. Did he quote Psalm li., or repeat what he remembered of the confession of the Prodigal Son? But if so, was he not stopped before he had gone far into either? Did he not hear that gentle voice calling for the best robe, the ring, the feast, the music, and song? Yes, we know all that passed. We have gone through it! We, too, have been lifted from the dust and made to sit at the King's table, though, like Mephibosheth, we have been "lame in both our feet."

What delicate thoughtfulness there was in the Master's arrangement of this personal interview prior to the later gathering of the day, when He revealed Himself to the entire company. In their presence Peter could never have poured out his soul, or made full confession, or have kissed His feet. That first hour of radiant fellowship cast its sheen on all subsequent hours of that memorable day. Having washed in the laver of forgiveness, he had boldness to enter into the Holiest; and when the Lord showed His hands and side, the credentials of His finished work, and breathed on them the zephyr-breath of Pentecost, Peter was able to appropriate them to the full.

What mortal tongue can tell or pen describe the delicacy, depth, tenderness, and strength of the love of Jesus? The thought has sometimes suggested itself whether it was not worth being born of a sinful race to have had the opportunity of learning what the forgiving grace of Jesus is. Charles Kingsley desired that these three words should be engraved on the tomb which held the mortal remains of his wife and himself—*Amavimus, Amamus, Amabimus*—we loved, we love, we shall love. But the love of Jesus in its past, present, or future, only eternal ages will reveal.

Yet why do we speak of tenses, when we speak of God's Love? It is eternal, ageless, timeless. Before time began, and when time has ceased to be, Love *is*. We may compare the sun with the glow-worm's torch, but each has had its beginning and will have its close; whilst the Love of Jesus has neither the one nor the other. Fear not! It will never fail thee!

XVI

THE RENEWED COMMISSION

JOHN xxi.

"And man's forgiveness may be true and sweet,—
But yet he stoops to give it! More complete
Is Love that lays Forgiveness at thy feet,
And pleads with thee to raise it! Only Heaven
Means crowned, not vanquished, when it says 'Forgiven!'"

A. Procter.

IT IS almost certain that the final chapter of John's Gospel—which has been described as a postscript—was appended by the beloved Apostle as a tribute to the memory of his friend, who, according to universal tradition, had sealed his long and glorious ministry by martyrdom— the martyrdom of the Cross. In noble loyalty to Peter's memory, he desired to show how, notwithstanding the three-fold denial, the Lord had Himself replaced the keys in his hand and returned his sword. The Primitive Church had already recognized him as one of its pillars; but the story of his actual rehabilitation had not been placed on the canvas of history. Accordingly, beneath the inspiration of the Divine Remembrancer, the Apostle-Evangelist set himself to paint his inimitable scene, the exquisite naturalness and beauty of which attest its authenticity.

Is there one of us who has not been entangled in some word and act which, if taken by itself, might have been interpreted as debarring us from future service in the Flock of Christ? But we knew in our deepest soul that such an interpretation would have been absolutely erroneous and unjust, since we were conscious that the failure was an exception, not the rule; an eddy or cross-current on the surface, not the main drift of the stream. Of course, there are sudden outbursts of evil which reveal an inward rottenness of long duration, as the fall of a forest-tree may result from the prolonged activity of the borer-worm at its heart. We must not forget to make that admission;

but it is also true that under strong and sudden pressure a man may be betrayed into acts and words which belie his true self, as Peter's oaths, in the hall of Annas, belied his faithful attachment to the person of his Lord.

All things are naked and open to the eyes of Him with whom we have to do. Jesus knew that the Peter of the denial was not the real Peter, and since his future leadership depended on the concurrence of his brethren, He skilfully contrived to bring about a revelation of Peter's innermost soul, that the effect of his denial might be neutralized, and that unquestionable proof might be afforded of his possession of the qualities required for the leadership of the Church. The great Architect of the Church knew the qualities of the man who was to be the Master-Builder, and took care to provide the platform on which their possession by Peter would be displayed. The unanimity with which his leadership was agreed to proves the infinite wisdom which inspired the Lord's action when they met for the last time on the shores of the Lake of Galilee.

I. The Scene.—In obedience to their instructions, the Apostles returned to Galilee and to the Lake, every headland and inlet of which was fragrant with hallowed associations. Here He wrought that miracle! Yonder He was sitting when He spoke those words! Their circumstances, however, were entirely different. The funds, which our Lord shared with them, were no longer forthcoming; and as the time of their next interview was unknown, and a long interval might elapse before they received further instructions, they were prepared to adopt Peter's proposal to resume their former craft. Simon Peter said, "I go a-fishing." They immediately agreed with his suggestion, and replied, "We also come with thee."

The evening breeze was fragrant with the myriad flowers of spring. Meadows and mountain-pastures were aglow with colour. The Lake lay dimpling in the warm sunset. Boats and nets were to hand; and with the eager alacrity with which men will respond to the call of an old-time but long-discarded habit, seven of them pushed off from shore in one of the larger fishing-boats, a smaller one being attached to the stern, and made off for the familiar fishing-grounds. Darkness stole down the mountains, the lights died out along the shore, heaven's vault revealed its starry galaxies, the silence of the night was broken only by the letting-out and drawing-in of the nets, or the occasional stroke of the oar; but when the grey morning began to break—they had taken nothing.

The disappointment was hard to bear. But those who have had experience of God's dealings are well aware that one door is shut that another may be opened, and that our programme is arrested in a certain direction because God has provided something wiser and better. Had the fishers been successful that night, it would have been much more difficult to win them back to a life of dependence on their Master's personal care. He wished them to understand that their livelihood was to be obtained, not by plying their fishing-craft, but by fires that He would light and meals that His own hands would prepare. The lesson is for us all. If our days are filled with consecrated service, we may go to our beds and sleep in peace. " It is vain to rise up early, and so late take rest, for so He giveth to His beloved in sleep."

They failed to recognize the Figure standing on the white, sandy shore, enwrapped in the golden shimmer of the morning mist. Surely He was some early fish-dealer; and the two inquiries addressed to them across the quiet water failed to dissipate their mistake. That fishermen, returning from a night of toil, should be asked if they had fish to sell, or that directions should be given for catching a shoal by one standing on the shore, were familiar incidents. But John, with the unerring instinct of love, discerned the presence of the Lord, and in a whisper passed his glad discovery to Peter. None of the others could, for the moment, have understood why he suddenly caught up and wrapped around his person the outer coat, which he had cast aside to expedite his labours, and plunged into the water, regardless of the morning chill. Those swift strokes, however, gave him a brief additional opportunity of lonely personal intercourse with Jesus, in which to renew the ecstasy of the Garden interview.

We may not linger on the tender, almost womanly, thoughtfulness which had kindled a fire, at which exhausted fishermen might chafe their limbs and dry their clothes, and which had prepared the bread and fish. Nor may we dwell on the frugality of the miraculous, which bade them bring of the fish that they had caught. It is enough if we learn from the entire incident that, from our Lord's Resurrection and onwards, the seine-net of the Gospel must be cast into the multitudinous waters of the human world, that the Master's presence and direction are absolutely essential to success, that the fisher's needs for comfort and subsistence would never be forgotten, and that when the Master and they have wrought together in obtaining the harvest of the sea, He will welcome them as they near the heavenly shore in the daybreak, and will feast with them and they with Him. None of them will then ask, Who art Thou? for they shall know that it is the Lord, and there shall be no misunderstanding or division, for the sea and morning mists will be no more, and the former things will have passed away.

The outstanding qualification for religious leadership are three: Passionate Devotion to Christ, Unfeigned Humility, and Indomitable Courage. In each of these Peter had been proved deficient by the incidents of the Betrayal-night. But they were latent in his soul, as clover-seed in an ill-nourished field, and only waited for favourable circumstances to call them forth. These circumstances and conditions were furnished by the Saviour's loving thoughtfulness.

(1) *Passionate Devotion to Christ.*—Had it not been for the Denial, none of the Apostolic band would have questioned Peter's attitude toward the Master. The members of the other groups must often have longed for the ardour of the Boanergic group, and especially of Simon Peter. But a shadow of grave doubt now overspread the sky, and as they spoke together they may have questioned, with all seriousness, the strength and steadfastness of his devotion. Our Lord realized this, and knew that before He entrusted to him the tendance of His sheep and lambs, He must secure a very decisive and unquestionable expression of the Love which He at least recognized as a dominant factor in His Apostle's character.

When, therefore, breakfast was over, Jesus repeated the same question thrice: "Lovest thou me?" and in each case addressed him as Simon Bar-Jona, i.e., Simon, son of John. "We read of one of the Caliphs," says Dr. Trench, "who gave to his principal officers an honourable surname suggested by their qualities. When he wished to show his dissatisfaction, he dropped it, calling them by their own names; this caused them great alarm. When he resumed the employment of the surname, it was a sign of their return to favour." This helps us to understand why our Saviour laid this stress on His servant's earlier name. He desired to give him a fresh opportunity of acquiring the Rockman title.

Love to Jesus is the indispensable qualification of service. Only those who love can satisfy the requirements of Christ's service. Only they can bear the fret and strain of wayward wills and faltering resolve. Love is needed for the gathering of tired and sick-lambs to the shepherd's bosom, for the weary mothers finding the mountain-path steep and difficult, and for the straying sheep, possessed by an incessant tendency to break through gaps, or wander browsing on forbidden pastures. The first, second, and third qualification of the true Shepherd is Love. Therefore the Master asked persistently, "Dost thou love Me?" And to the thrice-repeated question Peter returned the same reply, "Thou knowest that I love Thee," only adding at the third time: "Thou knowest it not only with the perfect knowledge of God, but with the intuitive sympathy of man."

If we may so state it, Peter showed great dexterity in using our Lord's silence to secure his vindication. In each case he put Christ in such a position that He must have broken silence had it not been so. He could not have held His peace, if He had entertained any doubt of Peter's passionate attachment to His Person and devotion to His service. This seems to have been the gist of Peter's reply. He staked everything on his Lord's intimate knowledge of the thoughts and intents of his heart, and challenged Him to refute his threefold avowal of love, if it was not true to fact. In after-days, when the Apostles discussed this remarkable incident, they must have acknowledged that they were convinced, not only by Peter's own statements, but because the Master, when He was appealed to, tacitly assented that they were true, and, by immediately repeating His commission, endorsed and confirmed them. Clearly the Master had no doubt about His servant's loyalty, or He would never have entrusted him with responsibilities so arduous and important. There is much comfort here. The Lord knows all things. The tiny lichen on the stone, the limpet on the rock, the ephemeræ of the forest glade! All are within His vision, and so also is our love, though often overgrown, confused in utterance, and blushing to confess Him.

(2) *Unfeigned Humility.*—Two Greek words stand for Love. The one expresses the reverent and adoring Love with which we should regard the Holy God. The other expresses love in its more human

and affectional aspect. In His two first questions, Jesus asked His Apostle whether he loved with the former love. This Peter modestly disclaimed. "Nay," said he, "but I love Thee with the ardour of personal affection." Finally, our Lord descended to his level and asked if indeed he loved Him thus, eliciting the immediate response: "Assuredly, and whether as Son of God or Son of man, Thou knowest it right well."

With evident reference to Peter's boast made at the Supper, that though his fellow-disciples might desert the Master, yet he never would, Jesus asked him if he loved Him more than the rest. But all his braggart boastfulness had gone, and he, by his silence and his grief, confessed that he dared not claim any priority in love. He was prepared to take the lowest seat, and own himself last and least. In this, also, he proved that he was worthy for the foremost place, because he was willing to take the lowest. If only he might fill some lowly office he would be content. He had become as a little child; and our Lord did not hesitate, with the hearty assent of the brethren who stood around, to take him by the hand and place him in the old foremost position which he seemed to have forfeited for ever.

(3) *Indomitable Courage.*—From the beginning our Lord saw the Cross standing clear-cut on the horizon before Him. Amid all the excitement of His early appearance, He told Nicodemus that the Son of man must be lifted up. Do we sufficiently estimate His courage in treading resolutely a path that led ever deeper into the valley of death? Not for a moment would we depreciate the magnificent courage with which, in the excitement of the charge, the soldier flings himself on the foe, foot to foot, steel to steel. But we may fairly question whether it will bear comparison with courage of that other quality which, with the certain knowledge of a most terrible death before it, never flinches, never loses its self-composure or genial kindliness, but continues to pursue the course which will inevitably incur that fate, the anticipation of which freezes the blood.

This was our Lord's experience. "I have a baptism to be baptized with, and how am I straitened till it be accomplished?" Henceforth it was to be Peter's also. "Thou shalt stretch forth thy hands, and another shall gird thee, and carry thee whither thou wouldst not. This, He said, signifying by what death he should glorify God." In his proud self-confidence Peter once said: "Lord, with Thee I am ready to go to prison and to death." The Saviour replied: "Thou canst not follow Me *now*, but thou shalt follow Me afterwards." This *afterwards* had now dawned. The disciple was not to be above his Lord. He was to follow Him to prison in Acts xii., and to death at the end of all—the death of the Cross, as tradition assures us, and this prediction suggests. In his second Epistle Peter refers to these words of Jesus: "I know that the putting off of my Tabernacle cometh swiftly, even as our Lord Jesus signified unto me." Clearly for him also the Cross was the ultimate goal; but he never swerved from the chosen path of service because of its menace. He was steadfast and unmovable, always abounding in the work of the Lord. For the joy that was set before him, he was willing to endure the Cross, despising the shame, and for him also there was laid up a crown of righteousness. The courage that could stand that strain was of rare and splendid quality, and approved his fitness for leadership.

By evincing his ownership of these three qualities Peter established his right to the foremost place in the glorious company of the Apostles, and he nobly fulfilled the position, as we shall see. He would have been glad if John's companionship and help had been granted him, and this yearning for his fellowship inspired the question, "What shall this man do?" But other work awaited the beloved Apostle, and would take him in another direction. "No," said our Lord, "John cannot be spared to you, but I will be your all-sufficient Helper to the end." What that companionship meant for Peter is made clear in his epistles, especially in the verse which tells us that he rose to the highest form of love, the form which he had not dared to claim. "Whom not having seen ye love," not only with the love of passionate affection, but with that of the highest quality—the love of God Himself.

XVII

A WITNESS OF THE RESURRECTION

Acts i. 1–26; ii. 1–11.

" Then robing Him in viewless air, He told
His secret to a few of meanest mould:
They in their turn imparted
The gift to men pure-hearted,
While the brute many heard His mysteries high,
As some strange fearful tongue, and crouch'd—they knew not why."
Newman.

WITH HIS brethren Peter returned from the scene of the Ascension to the city with great joy. Though he must have realized that the blessed intercourse of the last six weeks was now ended, and that his Master had definitely gone to the Father, yet the indubitable evidence of His great power and glory, the memory of those hands outstretched in benediction as He went, the assurance that they were to be endued with the power of the Comforter within the next few days, and the assurance that Jesus when He came again, as He certainly must, would be the same unchangeable Lord and Friend as they had known Him, were sufficient to lift them all into an ecstasy of joy and triumph, which exceeded and overflowed their sense of deprivation. It was even as He had said, their Master had not left them comfortless.

Quite naturally they returned to *the* Upper Room, hallowed by so many precious associations. It may have been part of the house of the mother of John Mark, which afterwards became the gathering-place for the harried Church; and probably it was filled to its utmost capacity when the entire group of Apostles, disciples, holy women, and the brethren of the Lord, was assembled. Peter seemed naturally and by universal consent to become their leader; but there is no sign of the autocratic power with which some would invest him. He simply acted as chairman or moderator for the time being, because the Lord Himself, though unseen, was recognized by them all as still literally present; and it was to Him that the choice between the two candidates for the Apostolate was referred. "Do thou, Lord, who knowest all hearts, show which of these two Thou hast chosen." It must have been with intense inward emotion that Peter compared his own position, as the honoured leader of the assembly, with the lot of Judas, whom he had known so intimately. How he must have secretly wondered at and adored the grace which had saved him from taking his own life in that hour of awful anguish, when he too realized that he had failed his Lord in the supreme crisis! The difference between the two men lay in this that the one acted designedly and deliberately, whilst the other—to use the words of another Apostle— was overtaken by a sudden gush of temptation against which he had made insufficient preparation.

The one particular on which we lay stress is the definition which Peter gave of the special work which lay before them, as it had been outlined by the Lord during the previous days. They were to be witnesses to the fact of the Resurrection of their Lord. His words are very definite. "It is necessary," he said, "that of the men who have been associated with us from the beginning of our Lord's ministry in the days of John the Baptist until now, one must be chosen to become *with us* a witness to His Resurrection." When their Master had said that they were to be His witnesses, Peter perceived that the one outstanding fact on which their witness-bearing must be concentrated was His Resurrection, that carried with it all the rest and was the keystone to their position.

I. THE SALIENT FEATURE OF PETER'S LIFE-WORK.—It was witness-bearing to the Resurrection. The word translated witness is fraught with solemn and sacred associations. It is *martyr*. So many of the early witnesses sealed their testimony with their blood, that the word became synonymous with the yielding up of life amid the horrors of fire and sword, of the prison-cell and the amphitheatre. We cannot utter the word lightly. It is significant of tears, and blood, and death-agony, and the light reflected from the face of Jesus on the death pallor of upturned faces.

The Resurrection of Jesus is not primarily to be argued for as a doctrine; it rests on attestation to a fact. It is, indeed, a gospel, a theology, and a philosophy. It was the fitting consummation of the work of Jesus. It satisfies the heart, answers our deepest longing, and harmonizes with the silent analogies of nature. It is consistent with the anticipations of the Prophets, which have been since the world began. But, primarily, it is an historical fact, communicated and vouched for by a sufficient number of unimpeachable witnesses.

There is a vast difference, therefore, between the arguments on which Plato and others based their belief in the immortality of the soul and our belief in the Resurrection of the Christ. That the soul would live after this brief span of life, like as the bird might flit through a rudely-constructed banqueting-hall, entering from out the stormy darkness at the one end, and, after flying through the lighted chamber, issuing forth again into the night, that there must be a judgment, a weighing, a readjustment of the unequal lots of human life—these and similar processes of reasoning established the strong probability of life hereafter, which impressed Egyptians, Greeks, and Anglo-Saxons. But, at the best, it was only a probability. In the Resurrection of Jesus men were confronted with a fact, which could not be gainsayed, in that the resurrected body of Jesus was "seen for many days of them that came up with Him from Galilee to Jerusalem, who became His witnesses to the people." There is a clear distinction, therefore, between the Platonic philosophy which argues for Immortality, and the Christian faith in the Resurrection, which, as a well-attested fact, has brought Life and Immortality to light. "We are witnesses," said Peter and the others, "that the God of our fathers hath raised up Jesus, whom ye slew, hanging Him on a tree." This was his testimony on the Day of Pentecost; and in the house of Cornelius, when he was used to unlock the door of faith to the Gentiles, he said: "Him God raised up on the third day, and shewed Him openly; not to all the people, but unto witnesses chosen by God, even to us, who did eat and drink with Him after He rose from the dead."

II. PETER'S EQUIPMENT FOR HIS LIFE-WORK.—Before our Lord entered on His ministry He was anointed with the Holy Spirit, and from the wilderness He returned in the power of the Spirit into Galilee. May we not say that He also tarried till He (so far as His human nature required it) was endued with power from on high?

That was our Saviour's Pentecost. What was true of the head must be also true of the body. The sacred oil must descend to the hem of the garments of the High Priest. If He was the Christ, i.e., the Anointed, how much more must His followers stoop beneath the chrism of Pentecost, that they might truly be known as Christians, i.e., anointed ones!

This is what He had promised. He said: "I go to the Father, and will ask of Him, on your behalf, and He will give you another Paraclete, that He may abide with you for ever, even the Spirit of Truth." Having therefore, passed through the heavens, and taken His seat at the right hand of God, He did not fail of His sure promise, but asked and received of the Father into His Divine human nature, that fulness of the Holy Spirit, which had been His in His pre-existent glory, but which now, as the Head of the Church, He was able to pour forth upon all who were united with Him by a living faith.

Day after day they waited, sometimes in the Upper Room, but perhaps more often, as Luke tells us, in the Temple, worshipping Christ, blessing God with great joy, and wondering how soon, and in what manner, the promised gift of power would be bestowed. How often must they have quoted and pondered those parting words— "Ye shall receive power by the Holy Spirit coming upon you." But they all continued together in prayer, with the women, and Mary, the blessed mother, and His brethren. Each day they expected, but for ten days patience was given the opportunity of perfecting her work.

It was the first day of the week, and a notable day withal, for the priests in the special Temple service would present the first loaves of the new harvest before God. That the fulness of the year had been safely gathered in was the subject of universal congratulation and thankfulness. The city was crowded with people from all the world. It was a time of house decoration, festal dresses, jubilant processions. "How great was His goodness and how great His beauty, corn made the young men cheerful, and the new vintage the maids." It was the early morning, the embryo Church was probably assembled in one of the courts or precincts of the vast Temple area. They were all together in one place, when there was a sound from Heaven, as of the rushing of a mighty wind, which startled the entire city; and there appeared what seemed to be a globe of fire, which broke into tongues as of flame, that rested on each of them. Peter looked on John, and saw the expressive symbol on his bowed head, little realizing that the same sublime event had also happened to himself. Then looking around, and seeing each similarly crowned, he concluded that an equal share in this fiery baptism had been imparted to him also. Perhaps he at that moment remembered the words of his first teacher: "There cometh One after me, who is mightier than I, whose sandals I am not worthy to unloose, He shall baptize you in the Holy Spirit and in fire." The whole company were filled, and began to speak with other tongues, as the Spirit gave them utterance—Peter with the rest.

Meanwhile, summoned by the extraordinary sound, which evidently emanated from the Temple, a vast motley crowd gathered. It was composed of Jews and proselytes, religious men, gathered from every part of the known world. The East, as far as Media, the North to the borders of the Caspian, the West from the coast-lands of Egypt and Lybia, and Rome, the world's metropolis, had furnished contingents. As this torrent of excited and questioning multitudes poured into the Temple area, they were accosted by the newly-anointed disciples, who, with an assurance which their new experience had given, went freely amongst them, attesting the risen glory of Him whom their rulers had recently rejected and nailed to the cross. One of them accosted a Jew from Greece, and in the purest Attic, told him that Christ had risen. Another met a Jew who had, by residence in Rome, acquired the right of citizenship, and told the story of Jesus in language that Cicero or Horace could not have excelled. A third encountered a group which, by their dress, had evidently hailed from Arabia, and poured into their astonished ears the Gospel story.

Then Peter stood up and began to speak. His sermon was little else than the citation of long passages of Scripture, accompanied by brief comments, showing their application to the present hour; but the effect was extraordinary. As this Galilean fisherman began to speak, the mob suddenly became a congregation, the stormy waves of tumultuous emotion dropped into a calm, the minds of the audience were penetrated and subdued by the speaker's fervid eloquence, and the crowd became as one body, swayed and inspired by a common impulse. Presently the silence was broken by the cry as of a man who was mourning for his firstborn, and it was met by the wailing as of a woman for an only child. The hearers were convulsed in tears, and sobs, and panic of soul, and from the entire congregation the entreaty arose: "Men and breathren, what shall we do?"

That anointing or infilling came to Peter at least twice afterwards, for the Scripture so teaches, but probably it came again and again. He was filled with the Holy Spirit on the Day of Pentecost, and a second time when he addressed the Court, and was filled again on returning with John from the presence of the Sanhedrim to their own company. Why, then, should we go on year after year without claiming our share in this Pentecostal Power? The manufacturers in our cities are not content with the processes and machinery which sufficed for their fathers, but are ever pressing forward to avail themselves of every fresh invention for the saving of waste and the securing each fresh development of the hidden forces of Nature. First, they discarded hand-power for steam; then steam for electricity, and now electricity for the ether. They are set on obtaining the highest available power to drive their factories. Ah, why do we fail to make use of that vast spiritual dynamic of which Pentecost was the specimen, and the key of which is in the hands of our risen Lord, who waits to open that which no man can shut, though He shuts to all who refuse to employ the one pass-word or pass-key of Faith! We are not straitened in God, but in ourselves. We have not, because we ask not, or because we ask amiss.

The promise is to us, to our children, and to all that are far off— this is the special phrase by which Gentile believers are known—even as many as the Lord our God shall call. Thus the blessing, originally confined to Jews, may become the heritage of Gentiles also who believe in Christ. They also may receive the Holy Spirit through faith. There is not a single believer who reads this page who may not claim a share in the Pentecostal gift. The Spirit may be *in* us, regenerating and renewing from within, as Jesus was born of Mary through the Spirit; but it is necessary that He should be *on* us also, as He descended and remained on Jesus in His Baptism, if we are to fulfil our ministry to mankind. No learning, no polished speech, no amount of Evangelical teaching short of the Holy Spirit can avail for preaching the Gospel to the poor, the healing of the broken-hearted, the deliverance of the captive, and the recovering of sight to the blind. We must learn to say with Jesus, "The Spirit of the Lord is upon Me, and He hath anointed Me." Why not acknowledge that there is a blessing here, which is yours by right, but not yours by possession? Why not confess that it is your failure and fault not to have claimed it? Why not search out, confess, and be delivered from the sin or unbelief that has deprived you of your purchased possession? Why not humbly open your heart to the entrance of that blessed Spirit who changes the craven-hearted into courageous confessors, and makes the weakest mighty as the Angel of the Lord?

III. THE CHARACTERISTICS OF PETER'S LIFE-WORK OF WITNESSING. —*It was persistent.* On the day of Pentecost in Acts ii.; in his next great address, on the healing of the lame man in iii.; in his apology before the rulers, elders, priests, and scribes in iv. 10; by the great power with which he gave witness to the Resurrection of the Lord Jesus, in iv. 33; in his second conflict with the Council in v. 32; in the answer which he gave to the inquiries of Cornelius and his friends in x. 39–41—Peter was constantly and consistently a witness to the same outstanding fact that though Jesus was crucified through weakness, yet He was living through the power of God.

Thus, when many years had passed, and he was inditing his last messages to the strangers scattered throughout the regions represented on the Temple plateau when the Spirit was first outpoured, we are not surprised to find him saying that the God and Father of our Lord Jesus Christ had begotten him and others unto a living hope by the resurrection of Jesus Christ from the dead, and also that emergence from the waters of baptism was a symbol of the rising of the body of Christ from the grave to the right hand of God, angles, authorities, and powers being made subject unto Him.

It was steeped in Scripture quotation. We have already noticed this in the Pentecostal sermon, where out of twenty-two verses in the A.V., twelve are taken up with quotations from the Prophets and Psalms. We meet with the same feature in the next chapter, where he refers twice to the predictions of the holy Prophets, that it behoved the Christ to suffer, and to rise from the dead the third day. It seemed as though a very special illumination had been given him by the Holy Spirit of Inspiration, that he might understand the Scriptures and perceive the relevance to Jesus of all things written in the Law of Moses, the Prophets, and the Psalms.

This is always the case. The Spirit bears witness to the Word. The Testimony of Jesus is the Spirit of Prophecy. When the God of our Lord Jesus Christ communicates to the soul of man the Spirit, who proceeds from the Father and the Son, He becomes the Spirit of Wisdom and understanding in the knowledge of the Scriptures, and they become as a field of the cloth of gold, in the sheen of His uprising; or as the serried range of the Bernese Oberland at dawn and sunset. Spirit of the Risen Lord, open our eyes, we beseech Thee, that we may see the face of Christ reflected in every Scripture, as in a mirror, now darkly, but which one day we shall see face to face!

It grew in clearness of perception. As one climbs a mountain the view extends. Ravishing glimpses of other solemn heights, of wooded slopes, of verdant pastures, of the utmost ocean-rim, where the sunlight sparkles, break successively on the eye. Thus it is with the Spirit's revelation of Jesus! Peter begins with "the Man of Nazareth approved of God." Then "Lord and Christ." Then "Jesus Christ of Nazareth." Then "His Son Jesus." Then the "Holy One and the Just." Then the extraordinary sublime phrase is piled as a climax and top-stone on all the rest—"the Prince of Life."

Prince! He is royal, and deserves the homage of all the living. Prince of Life! There is a world, beyond the range of sense, where all live, and live unto Him! Prince of Life! In the literal rendering of this great word He is the Author and Giver of Life, so that he who believes in Him, though he has died, yet shall he live; whilst he that liveth and believeth in Him shall never die. Prince of Life! All hail! Let us count all things but dross that we may win the full-orbed knowledge of the Son of God, beneath the tutelage and guidance of the Holy Spirit. Let us leave behind us all we have known of Him, and press on to know Him, and the power of His Resurrection. Let us count all things but loss for the excellency of the knowledge of Christ Jesus our Lord. Even if the Divine Teacher may have to place us at points of suffering or deprivation in order to give us fresh aspects of the knowledge of the Son of God, let us not complain, for the heart of man has never entered into the full apprehension of Christ unless it has learnt to be conformed to Him in His death. The merchantman found himself well repaid when he carried away the pearl of great price, though he had parted with everything to get it.

It was based on present experience. It is remarkable that in Peter's witness to the Master's Risen Life he does not refer to the spectacle of the empty grave, the ordered clothes, the Garden interview, the vision of His hands and side, the breakfast by the Lake, or the Ascension from Olivet. He says: You may judge for yourselves by *this,* "*which ye now see and hear.*" In other words, he felt that not only was Jesus on the other side of the thin veil, which hides the unseen world, but that He was doing things. He had reached the Father's right hand, and was sending the Spirit, as He promised. He was empowering them with boldness, insight, and utterance. He was working with them, and confirming their words with signs following. He was making lame men walk, prison-doors open, hard hearts to break. Jacob could hardly have been convinced, if his sons had confined themselves to affirming that they had seen Joseph in Egypt, but when they brought the old man out to view the wagons that Joseph had sent—wagons of Egyptian manufacture, oxen such as only Egypt could breed—the patriarch was satisfied and exclaimed: "Joseph is yet alive. This is just what I might have expected of him. I will go and see him before I die." Peter said: "He whom ye delivered up and denied in the presence of Pilate, is alive, of this we all are witnesses, and *so is also the Holy Spirit.*" Thus the testimony of those early witnesses came not only in power, but in much assurance. When they affirmed that Jesus died and rose and lived, the Holy Paraclete corroborated with His affirmation. "*Yea,* saith the Spirit." He stood beside them, not only convincing men of sin, righteousness and judgment, but showing wonders in heaven above, and signs in the earth beneath; "blood, and fire, and vapour of smoke."

Similarly a holy life will corroborate our witness to the living Christ. If contrary to our former habit we seek the things which are above; if we manifestly derive from an unseen source the power that overcomes the world; if our joy abounds in pain and sorrow, like springs of fresh water amid the ocean; if though poor, we make many rich, being hated, we love, being refused, we entreat, being crucified, we invoke forgiveness on the agents of our shame—we prove that Jesus lives; like Stephen we must say: "Behold I see heaven opened and the Son of man standing"; and the angel-look on our faces must corroborate our words.

We know that Jesus suffered under Pontius Pilate, was crucified and buried, but the sources of our life do not spring from the hole dug on Calvary to receive His cross. We are not called to live always in the far-off scenes, of His agony and death. We do not need the aqueduct of the unbroken witness-bearing of the Church to conduct to us the blood which is life indeed. We have direct and immediate fellowship with the Prince of Life. The life that left His heart a moment ago is now beating in our pulses. The purposes that are forming in His thought and becoming energized by His will are ours also. We have the mind of Christ. The prayers which He is offering beside the golden altar are the much incense which makes our own intercessions acceptable. We speak of things that we know, and testify of things we have seen. That which we have seen, and handled, in our own experience, are what we communicate.

If only we, who profess the Name of Jesus, would tarry at His doors until he gave us audience, as Esther did in the palace of Ahasuerus, we should go to men with His accent on our tongues, and His light upon our hearts, and they would be compelled to admit that such witness could only be accounted for on the hypothesis that within the veil stood One whom they knew not.

But why should we not? We are called to stand within the Holy Place. Behind us the remnants of the torn veil, and before, the glory of God in the face of Jesus. With unveiled face we are called upon to behold and reflect that glory. Let us not abdicate from our high privilege. Let us not allow systems of doctrine, ritual, or service, or even our efforts after a sanctified life, to come between us and the direct vision of the Risen One. Then we shall issue forth upon the world bearing such evident traces of a life that cannot be accounted for, that those who know us best will be compelled to look from us to Him who lives for evermore. The light on the opaque surface of the moon, which has no lustre of her own, attests beyond contradiction the existence of the sun, though we see him not; and as we live in conference with Christ, we shall be witnesses of His Resurrection, and secure the co-witness of the Yea of Pentecost.

XVIII

"IN THE NAME"

ACTS iii. 16.

"O strengthen me, that while I stand
Firm on the Rock and strong in Thee,
I may stretch out a loving hand
To wrestlers with the troubled sea."

F. R. Havergal.

"HIS NAME through Faith is His Name." These two are inseparable. The Name, i.e., the Nature of Jesus, may be poured forth as fragrance on the air, or light from the sun, but there must be an appropriate organ of sense ready, or the fragrance will be wasted and the light unappreciated. Before perfect soundness can be imparted to any bruised, lame, or helpless soul, there must be the energy of the Divine, which resides in Jesus, and the receptivity of the Human, which is the necessary condition in us. No great work of salvation or renewal is possible apart from the clear enunciation of preacher, teacher, or Christian worker, first of His Name, and second, of Faith in His Name. Not the Name without the Faith, and not the Faith apart from the Name, but the Name *and* Faith in the Name.

A landscape may be outspread before us, from the snow mountains on the horizon to the blue waters of the lake at our feet, but there must also be a healthy human eye! Truth may be explained with lucidity and eloquence, but of what service will expositors be apart from the intelligent and alert mind? Love may throb in the breast of the mother, but alas! if there be no response in the lad or girl who has drifted into some far country! Always there should be the Name and the organ of Faith in the Name. Beneath the teaching of the Holy Spirit Peter had learnt this lesson well, and in his second great Pentecostal sermon he announced and bequeathed the eternal truth that the Nature of the Risen Lord, appropriated of a living Faith, will give perfect soundness.

I. WHAT PETER SAW.—The Temple was enclosed in three marble courts, rising in successive levels from the city floor. The lowest of these was the only one open to Gentiles. A flight of steps led up from it to the second, or middle, court, beyond which women might not go. Thence another flight of steps ascended to the upper level on which were the altar and the sanctuary. At the head of this second stairway, which only Jewish men might ascend, stood the Beautiful Gate, which opened on the Temple level. It was made of Corinthian brass—an amalgam of precious metals formed at the burning of Corinth—and richly overlaid with plates of gold and silver, which in the sunrise shone with dazzling glory. The Temple entrance faced the East, to make sun-worship impossible, and therefore this magnificent doorway, fashioned after the semblance of a vine, was the first to catch the sunrise. It was so massive as to task the strength of twenty men to open and close its massive leaves. It was surely fitting that men should enter the Temple of God by the door of Beauty. We remember that the Psalmist sang of "the beauties of holiness." In nature God ever expresses Himself in forms of beauty. Whether it be the frosted devices that Winter imprints upon our window-panes, or the platines of cirri which lie on the blue meadows of the sky like a flock of resting sheep—all God's handiwork is naturally beautiful. When the Love of God is in our hearts, it will express itself in exquisite poetry, in richest architecture, and in music from which perhaps angel-minstrelsy may get the theme of new songs. This is not wrong, so long as we do not allow the outward and sensuous to overwhelm or submerge the devotion of the spirit. We may have our Gate Beautiful, but we must not stay there wondering at its beauty. If we do, it will become a snare and hurtful. We must pass through the outward to the inward, through the sensuous to the spiritual, through the emblem to the reality. Else it will be better that, like the early Puritans, we should carefully abjure the beautiful, and worship in the barest sanctuaries, with nothing to vie with the claims of the All-Holy, who dwells not in places made with hands.

For Beauty alone can never inspire Life or Health; and there was an evident example of its impotence—apart from the Spirit of Life— in the presence of this unfortunate man, now more than forty years of age, who from his birth had never walked, and who was so poor that he needed to live on charitable doles, to obtain which he was daily carried by kindly hands from the poor slum where he dwelt to that spot near the Beautiful Gate, on which he lay year after year, begging a pittance from the crowds that passed him through the Gate to gain the Temple plateau. He was evidently a well-known figure to the citizens who made constant visits to the sacred shrine. It is a tribute to the power of religion that poor people gather towards its fires, from the chill indifference of the world; but we must see to it that we do not rid ourselves of responsibility for them by a passing dole. It is wiser far to consider the cause of distress and poverty, and endeavour to remedy it, than to drop a meagre coin into the outstretched hand and pass away. It is not thus that we act as our brother's keeper.

As in company with his friend and fellow-Apostle Peter passed up the Temple steps on his way to the afternoon service, he beheld the glory of the magnificent structure in all its wealth, and his eye would have been attracted by the splendour of the gateway through which they were about to pass. He saw also the familiar spectacle of this lame man in his misery. But he saw something beside, which was hidden from unanointed eyes. Being in the Spirit, the secrets of the spiritual world were open to him, and he beheld that crippled life as God meant it to be—whole, sound, healthy, vigorous, full of the music of perfected human vitality. The ideal man was there hovering as a beautiful vision above the travesty that lay on that well-worn mat. The man who was presently to accompany them into the Temple, through that Beautiful Gate, "walking and leaping, and praising God," was there as a reality in the spiritual and eternal sphere, but awaiting realization in the actual experience of this material time-sphere.

He saw also the Prince of Life, nearer to him than breathing, closer than hands and feet. The Lord of the Temple was beside him, ready to co-operate, brimming with the power of an indissoluble life, yearning to communicate the strength and vigour so urgently needed by this crippled existence. Here was weakness, there immortal life. Here despair, there resource and hope. Here the depression of prolonged ill-health, there the radiance of the dawn. The one problem was to bring these two together. There must be His Name, but something more was necessary. Faith in His Name must be called unto operation before the lame man could obtain that perfect soundness, resident in the Prince of Life.

II. WHAT PETER DID.—The instant response given by the lame man to Peter's use of "the Name of Jesus Christ of Nazareth" suggests that it was the result of a long process of thought which had evidently been at work previously in the heart of the cripple.

Without doubt he was perfectly familiar with the person of Jesus of Nazareth. He had seen Him pass up those stairs scores of times. But He had no form nor comeliness, no appearance of affluent wealth, nothing to encourage the hope that He could give him an alms. The appearance of our Lord must have been that of the ranks from which he sprang. When they divided His clothes, the only thing that seemed of any worth to the soldiers was His inner tunic. But of late strange rumours had gathered around the Nazarene. All Jerusalem knew of His arrest, trial, and consignment to the Cross. The preternatural darkness that veiled His anguish and the earthquake which had synchronized with His death had been the subject of universal comment. The cripple himself was lying on the accustomed spot when the frenzied priests and Levites rushed out of the Temple Court with the tidings that the veil had been grasped and rent from top to bottom, as by unseen hands. The story of the empty tomb and of the mysterious disappearance on the Mount of Olives may also have been discussed in his hearing; and the recent marvel of the Day of Pentecost and its result had been matters within his own cognizance, for the Temple itself had witnessed them. He had heard the people talking as they came away from Peter's sermon; and the baptism of 3,000 converts in the great Temple reservoirs was too astounding not to have come to his ears. Thoughts of this kind had been floating for days through his mind. As yet they had not crystallized into resolve or action. They were waiting for some additional impulse before they would precipitate in a living and working faith. In the story of the Apostle Paul we are told that a similar case to this was presented to him at Lystra. There also was a man, lame from his birth, who had never walked. The same heard Paul's address, and we are told that at its close the Apostle fixed his eyes on him—and the same Greek word is used there as here—and saw that he had faith to be healed.

The similarity between these two cases is too remarkable to be passed over, and we may infer that, led by a Divine prompting, the Apostle suddenly realized, by a gleam of incipient faith on the cripple's face, that he had faith unto salvation, and by his voice and gesture called it into expression. In an instant there were the blade, the ear, and the full corn in the ear.

One of our Lord's injunctions, when He sent the Apostles forth was: Get you no gold, nor silver, nor brass in your purses, and no wallet for your journey; and though that marching-order had been modified on the eve of His death, it is probable that it was still literally fulfilled, and the Apostles, like the rest, ate at a common table, provided from the common purse. It was literally true as Peter phased it: "Silver and gold have I none."

There are four classes of persons in the world:

1. The people who have neither silver nor gold nor anything else to give—these are the drift-wood on the ocean.

2. The people who have silver and gold, and no moral or religious property—these are the paupers of the universe.

3. The people who have neither silver nor gold, but, like Peter, they have vision, inspiration, faith, hope, and love—these are the rich-unto-God.

4. The people who have silver and gold, and withal the things which are honourable, just, pure, lovely, and of good report.

The Apostles belonged to the third of these classes. They were poor, yet making many rich, as having nothing, and yet possessing the key to the Divine treasuries. Silver and gold they had none. In this, as the Pope reminded Thomas Aquinas, his fancied successors have widely departed from his example; but they had, as Aquinas reminded the Pope, a power which cannot be passed down any line of mystical descent, and can only be received as the direct and in-dividual gift of the Holy Spirit.

Wealth is not the standard of worth. Mankind has been primarily beholden to those who have possessed little of this world's goods, but have abounded "in faith, and utterance, and knowledge, and in all earnestness, and in love." Through the poverty of Christ we have been enriched with all spiritual treasures and entitled to an inheritance that fadeth not away. There are bags in the heavens that wax not old, and treasures in the heavens that fail not, where no thief draweth nigh, neither moth destroyeth. Yonder a little girl is sobbing piteously on the grave of her mother! I am touched, and offer her a gold piece! She snatches it from my hand, flings it into the open grave, and continues to sob convulsively! What more can I do? That is all that I had to give, and it was unavailing! Presently a poor woman, in plain and shabby clothes, kisses the child, strokes the little head, presses her to her bosom, and comforts her with gentle crooning! See the eyes droop in sleep, and the little one is soothed and quieted! That woman had neither silver nor gold, but she possessed what was infinitely more precious, and that she gave without stint. This is what the world needs to-day. Would that men and women of all classes in society realized it, and instead of the giddy race for wealth and pleasure, would possess themselves of, and impart to others, treasures compared with which the mines of Crœsus offer a miser's dole.

In the present case Peter communicated the inspiration of his own strong faith in Jesus of Nazareth. He summoned him to act on such faith as he had. He called on things that apparently were not as though they were. He mingled a drop of his own soul-tincture into the clouded uncertainty and questioning of the cripple's soul, and it suddenly crystallized with the daring act of faith. He took him by the right hand and raised him up, as he had seen his Master raise up his wife's mother years before. Immediately the man's faith sprang into vigorous exercise. His feet and ankle-bones *received* strength. The life of the risen Lord was now able to enter his anæmic frame. His mortal body was quickened by the entrance and accession of the life of the Prince of Life, who was working together with His Apostle, given on the Mount of Ascension. "He sat down at the right hand of God. And they went forth, and preached everywhere, the Lord working with them, and confirming their word by signs following." As for the cripple, he entered with them into the Temple, from which his congenital deformity had always excluded him, according to Levitical precept, "walking, and leaping, and praising God; and all the people saw him walking and praising God : and they took knowledge of him that it was he which sat for alms at the Beautiful Gate of the Temple, and they were filled with wonder and amazement at that which had happened unto him."

III. How Peter Preached.—When the Temple service concluded, and the two left the upper court, descended the steps, and crossed the marble pavement to the double colonnade called Solomons' Porch, in which our Lord used to teach, and where the infant Church generally gathered in those early days, a vast concourse of people followed, and in reply to the buzz of questioning and the awestruck wonder of the crowd Peter delivered his second great address.

He turned the thoughts of his audience from John and himself to their Lord. It was not by their power or holiness that the man stood there before them whole, but by the act of Him whom they had denied in the presence of Pontius Pilate, overpowering his ardent wish to release Him. He charged them with preferring a murderer to God's Holy and Righteous One. He insisted that the evidence of Christ's Resurrection consisted not simply in the witness of those who had been in His company after He had left the grave, but in the fact of the miracle wrought on the impotent man, which was evident to them all. He admitted that they and their rulers had not recognized the Lord of Glory, or they would not have crucified Him; and from that point he branched out into an eager entreaty that they would repent and turn again that their sins might be blotted out.

It is very interesting to obtain this side-light on the action of the Jewish rulers and the Jewish crowds. They were blinded by prejudice and wounded pride. They were expecting the Messiah to come in Princely State, and never dreamt that the mean garb of the village carpenter concealed the glories of Immanuel. Such ignorance did not excuse their crime, but palliated it. It left them within the zone of penitence and pardon. In this Peter only followed the example of Jesus, who drew a distinction between the servant who knew and the servant who knew not his Lord's will, and who, when the nails first pierced His tender flesh, cried, "Father, forgive them, they know not what they do." There is clearly a difference for the sins of presumption and of ignorance. For the former there remaineth no further sacrifice for sin; in the latter we may count on mercy, if only like Paul we turn to Him, whom we had in our ignorance repelled and crucified afresh.

Peter assured them that this sin might be blotted out. The Oriental merchant keeps his accounts on little tablets of wax. On these, with the blunt point of the stylus or pencil, he makes the indented record of a debt, and when it is paid, with the blunt end of his instrument he flattens down the wax, so that all record of the debt is entirely

obliterated. If we erase a debt from our account-book, there is still
the trace of it having been there, but on the wax there is no trace
whatever. The handwriting that was against the debtor is entirely
blotted out. The sin is blotted out, as Isaiah puts it, as completely
as a wreath of cloud is blotted from the summer sky. What a vision
Peter had of the utterness and completeness of the Divine forgiveness!
Once he had hazarded the suggestion that seven times was the limit
to which forgiveness could go. Now he has entered into a more
adequate conception of the Love of God, which forget as it forgives,
and drops our sins when we confess into the fathomless depths of the
ocean of His Love. They shall no more be found or remembered or
mentioned for ever.

The arguments with which the speaker plied his audience were
very tender and enticing. He said that if only Israel repented of their
sin and recognized Jesus of Nazareth as the Holy One of God, times
of refreshing would come from the presence of the Lord, and these
are afterwards defined as the times of the restoration of all things,
whereof God has spoken by the mouth of His holy prophets. Sweet
is the lay of prophecy; too sweet not to be wronged by a mere mortal
touch!

" *Six thousand years of sorrow have well-nigh fulfilled*
Their tardy and disastrous course over a sinful world;
And what remains of this tempestuous state of human things
Is merely as the working of the sea before a calm
That rocks itself to rest. For He whose car the winds are
And the clouds the dust that waits upon His sultry march,
Shall visit earth in mercy, shall descend; and what sin's storms
Have blasted and defaced, shall with a smile repair !
Oh scenes surpassing fable and yet true ! Scenes of accomplished bliss
Which who can see, though but in distant prospect, and not feel
His soul refreshed by foretaste of their joy !"

Notice the two sendings of the Christ. He was sent in the first
Advent to bless His people, in turning them away from their ini-
quities; He will be sent a second time to bring on the Golden Age,
to set up His Kingdom, to put down all rule and authority and power,
until such time as that God shall be All-in-All, and the eternal

timeless era of blessedness shall be inaugurated. What radiant visions had broken upon the soul of this man who was accounted ignorant and unlearned by the religious leaders of his age, but to whom, according to his Master's promise, the Holy Spirit was showing things to come!

Ere we close this chapter shall we not apply to ourselves its lessons? May not we be included amongst those who have spent many years just outside the Gate of the Blessed Life, lame and needing to be carried by Pastors, Teachers, Helpers, but not able to walk and run in the way of Christ's commandments; hearing the music floating through the gate, but not able to join; living a Christian life at second-hand, or perhaps not having commenced it? Let all such dwell on the Love, the invitations, the salvation offered them in Jesus Christ. Let them not only hear His Name, let them also believe in that Name, so shall they rise to the full stature of the perfect life, realize the Divine ideal that waits within their reach, and go on their way walking, leaping, and praising God!

XIX

"YOU BUILDERS"

ACTS iv. 1–37.

" God spake, and gave us the Word to keep;
Bade never fold the hands, nor sleep
'Mid a faithless world; at watch and ward,
Till Christ at the end relieve our guard.
By His servant Moses the watch was set,
Though near upon cock-crow, we keep it yet."

Browning.

PETER was still addressing the hushed crowd which the healing of the crippled man had gathered. The sunset of the Western sky was casting long shadows, and forming a gorgeous back-ground to the Corinthian columns of Solomon's porch. Suddenly a band of officials moved quickly towards the congregation, threaded its way through the densely packed mass of people, and forcibly arrested the three men, whose presence seemed magnetic. There were priests, who detected in these unordained and unrecognized laymen serious rivals. There were Sadducees, the unbelieving sections of the literary class, who were disbelievers in the world of Spirit, and in the doctrine of a life after death—a sect not numerous, but wealthy, powerful, and holding the chief offices of State. There was also the Captain of the Temple, with his band, charged with the duty of maintaining public order.

Probably the Sadducean party was chiefly responsible for this ill-timed and unpolitic act. Clearly they had special reasons for resenting the teaching, with which for days past the Apostles had been flooding Jerusalem. "They were indignant that they taught the people and preached through Jesus the Resurrection of the dead." If the story, which was attested by Peter and his friends, were true, Sadduceeism was ended. It is probable, therefore, that this arrest was instigated by Annas and Caiaphas, and the other leaders of this

134

powerful party. Before Jerusalem was aware of what was happening, the Apostles and the healed man were clapped in prison, and messengers were hastening through the city to summon the members of the Sanhedrim to meet early on the following morning.

That night must have been to the imprisoned trio one of unspeakable emotion. This was the treatment their Master had taught them to expect. Clearly they were on the path which He had foreseen. It was an opportunity also of redeeming the cowardly desertion of the Betrayal-night. Peter remembered that he had vowed to follow Jesus to prison, and here was the chance of fulfilling his promise. The man, whose healing had led to this collision with the rulers, was taught the significance of these happenings, and he joined in the prayers and psalms with which they beguiled the sleepless hours. As to the morrow's trial, they had no anxiety, nor prepared a defence, for the words spoken three years before came freshly back to memory: "When you are brought before rulers and kings, do not premeditate what ye shall answer, for it shall be given you in that same hour. It is not ye that speak, but the Spirit of your Father that speaketh in you."

The Sanhedrim was the most venerable and authoritative assembly and court in the world. It represented the seventy elders chosen to assist Moses in his administration of the Exodus march. The High Priest presided, and around him in a semicircle sat the heads of the twenty-four priestly classes, the doctors of the law, and the fathers of ancient Jewish families. The names of some of these are given, such as the crafty Annas, the unscrupulous Caiaphas, his son-in-law, the celebrated John Ben Zakkai, and Alexander, the wealthy brother of the learned Philo. It was the same body that had handed Jesus of Nazareth to the Roman executioners, and now, in the same chamber, they were preparing, by one supreme effort, to stamp out the Galilean heresy. Note their procedure! It was idle to question the miracle—the healed man was standing there before them. They could not deny it. It was perilous to discuss the general question of the Resurrection, because on this matter there was a distinct cleavage between the Pharisees and the Sadducees, each party being strongly represented. But the point at issue was as to the Source of his healing. "In whose name and by what power." If Peter and his associates had ascribed the miracle to the mighty power of Jehovah, with the stories of Elijah's and Elisha's miracles in view, nothing more could have been said. But if it were attributed to some other name, the Apostles would bring themselves within the ancient prescription of death as sorcerers. If they ascribed it to Jesus, they would risk the infliction of the death that had already been inflicted on Him. But Peter was entirely oblivious to all questions of policy, and beneath the inspiration of the Divine Spirit, spoke thus: "Rulers of the people and Elders, you question us about the deed done to this cripple and ask how he was made whole—we take this opportunity of saying publicly to you and to the whole nation that it was wrought through the Name of Jesus Christ of Nazareth, whom ye crucified, but whom God raised from the dead. It is in Him that this man stands before you whole. You builders rejected Him, but none the less is He the headstone of the corner. Neither is there salvation by any other."

I. THE RIVAL BUILDERS.—The reference to this rejected headstone recalls an ancient tradition woven into the structure of Psalm cxviii. —the climax of the great national Hallel. We are told that when Solomon built his famous Temple, all the masonry was performed at a distance, so that there were neither hammers, axe, nor any tool of iron heard in the building during its erection. One day, in the earlier operations, a huge stone was delivered from the quarry, which bore evidence, in its unusual shape, that considerable care had been expended on it, but no one could suggest the precise place in the structure it was intended to fill. It was put aside as a misfit, and lay on the site unrecognized and useless. The winds blew over it scornfully, the birds chirped and perched on it irreverently, and most people forgot it. But when the building began to emerge above ground, and a corner or headstone was needed of a particular shape, in the builder's dilemma some one remembered the rejected stone, which, when it was placed in the gap, answered the need with perfect exactitude. The memory of this incident was, therefore, embalmed in the words: "The stone which the builders refused, the same is become the Headstone of the corner."

Isaiah also alludes to it: "Thus saith the Lord, Behold, I lay in Zion a stone, a tried stone, a precious corner-stone, and a sure foundation, in which if a man believeth he shall not make haste."

Our Lord also directly quoted it of Himself, when He clenched the moral of His Parable concerning the Wicked Husbandmen; and in after-years the Apostles of the Gentiles referred to it in addressing the Ephesian Church: "Built on the foundation of Apostles and Prophets, Jesus Christ Himself being the chief Corner-stone."

The position accorded to that Corner-stone in the national structure was the real cause of divergence in the Assembly. Two ideals confronted each other. The one group of builders was composed of that brilliant and powerful body which comprised all that was most illustrious in the Hebrew Commonwealth. The other group was represented by those two simple "unlearned and ignorant" men. The former refused the Stone, and covered it with neglect. The other made it the keystone of the structure, which was beginning to arise, and has since spread through the world.

They said that they could do without it. They had no use for it. Then Peter remembered what his Master had said, that if a man refused it, he would fall on it and be broken; or that it would fall on him, as a dislodged rock might fall on a shepherd tending his flock beneath, and grind him to powder. Therefore he insisted that there was no salvation for men or nations apart from Christ.

Of course, his primary reference was to the healing of the impotent man, who stood there saved and whole before their eyes. But there was more in his thought. Was it not clear that Israel was the real cripple, after all? Beneath the rude Roman power the nation lay there bound, prostrate, and powerless. It was crippled morally and and spiritually. The burning passion of prophets and psalmists had died down; and in its place were these warring sectarians. With profound insight that the Holy Spirit gave, Peter realized that they had cast aside the one divinely-given opportunity of rehabilitation and safety. If only the Jewish leaders and builders had been induced to acknowledge his Master and Lord, their national influence would have revived, and they would have become what God meant them to be, the religious leaders of mankind. There was no salvation in any other.

We may apply this nationally, ecclesiastically, and individually.

Nationally.—If a nation refuses to build according to the great truths that Jesus taught, exemplified, and died for, it is not destined to permanence, but must pass as all the great empires of the world—Assyrian, Babylonian, Persian, Grecian, and Roman—have passed, and become as the dust of the summer threshing-floor. The only hope of salvation for the State is to be built foursquare with the Gospel of the Son of man. There is salvation of a permanent description in no other expedient.

Ecclesiastically.—The Church which substitutes doctrinal formularies, the pomp and splendour of high ritual, or priest-craft, learning, or wealth, for a vital contact with Jesus Christ, the living Saviour, may enjoy a temporary success of popularity; but it is not destined to endure. It will find itself unable to command or lead in the march of the human race. It will be left behind like some gigantic vestige of the Ice-Age in the congealed floes of the past. The only salvation for any Church is in Union with Jesus Christ. He is never stagnant, but ever the same, living for evermore, and leading on the Ages to their consummation in God, as All-in-All.

Individually.—We all build from our childhood. Who of us has not built with wooden bricks in winter, and sand-castles on the sea-shore in summer? When older we build businesses, stories, tragedies, poems, pictures, systems of philosophy, fortunes, or statesmanships. Too many build to the neglect of Christ. They can do without Him— so they say. They have no need, no use for Him. But they cannot continue. For a while they flourish and grow up, but the wind passeth over them and they are gone, and the place thereof knoweth them no more. But he that doeth the will of God abideth for ever. The life which is foursquare with Christ and at right angles with His teaching and example will shine as the stars for ever and ever; but those who reject or neglect Him are like the chaff which the wind driveth away.

If one had a trumpet-voice, one would cry, "Jesus Christ alone can save." By His agony and bloody sweat, by His Cross and Passion, by His glorious Resurrection and Ascension, He has thrown wide the Gates of Salvation. All who accept Him and enter into union with Him become as Mount Sion, that cannot be moved, but abideth for ever. Jesus is the Rock. He is the living stone! He gives eternal life and unchanging stability! Elsewhere you may get philosophy, moral integrity, virtue, but there is no other name given under heaven and among men whereby we must be saved.

II. The Irrepressibility of the Christ Life.—As the Sanhedrim listened to these words, and watched the two Apostles closely, they were irresistibly reminded of Jesus. They were animated by His Spirit, and spoke as He had done. They took knowledge of them that they had been with Jesus. Not only had they associated with and absorbed Him during the three happy years, which had now passed, but He was living in their hearts, and pouring through them the spirit of His own glorious existence as the Prince of Life.

When the court was cleared, with a view to private conference, they confessed to each other that they dared not permit these men to continue to preach and teach. They could not deny the miracle or disprove the Resurrection, but they must take thought for themselves. When the Apostles were recalled they were strictly charged not to speak further in the name of Jesus. Their judges would have been glad to punish them, but this would so enrage the people that it could not be entertained. So they further threatened them and let them go.

But they might equally have bidden the morning light not to spread, or the bursting life of spring to restrain itself, or the incoming tide to turn away back to its heart. These men could do no other than bear witness to the things that they had heard and seen. Even if they had resolved in their own hearts that they would speak no more in His Name, His words would have been as a fire shut up in their bones, and they would have been weary of forbearing and unable to restrain themselves. Is not this what the Apostle meant when he said, in answer to the remonstrances and arguments of his friends: "The Love of Christ constraineth us"? Oh that we knew more of these irresistible impulses, like steam generated in a boiler that must move machinery or shiver the containing vessel! Oh for this Divine passion, which like an overflowing stream catches hold of the logs, lying high up on the banks, and hurries them downwards to the ocean!

III. THE ATTESTATION OF THE HOLY SPIRIT.—They returned to their own company, who had doubtless spent the intervening hours in prayer. With what welcomes were they received! How intensely their narrative was listened to! Then what an outburst of adoration and prayer! Such a meeting could only be held subsequently in the torchlight of the catacombs, the recesses of Alpine caves, or on the moors of Scotland in the days of Claverhouse, when similar circumstances threw back the struggling Churches on the everlasting arms. There was no entreaty that God would stay the persecutor or save their lives. The sole request was that they might have power to give an unfaltering testimony, and that God would stretch out His hand to heal, so that wonders and signs might be wrought in the Name of Jesus. If only that dear Name could be magnified, extolled, and revered, they would be content to suffer to the extreme of human anguish! Let Jesus Christ be praised! Let Him see of the travail of His soul! Worthy was the Lamb that was slain to receive honour, and glory, and blessing! Let victory be granted to the cause of the Divine Saviour!

Can we wonder at Heaven's response? The tremor of it shook the place, as before on the Day of Pentecost. There was a second infilling of the Holy Spirit; not now for the hundred and twenty only, but for them all. The evidence of it was in the Divine Love, which prompted the sharing of their goods and secured the forging of a Divine unity of sentiment.

Peter must have been overwhelmed as he saw what had transpired. Well enough he knew that it was not because of his own power and holiness that such results had been secured. In the splendour of that hour the blemishes and failures of his past must have stood out in their native deformity and evil. How could he have spoken and acted as he did? But how passing wonder had been the Lord's forbearing grace! What could he say, than to fall on his face, sobbing and confessing, "Not unto me, not unto me, but to Thy Name be all the glory. Thou hast redeemed and saved me. And Thou hast magnified Thy mercy above all Thy Name!"

XX

PETER'S DEEPENING EXPERIENCES OF THE HOLY SPIRIT

Acts iv. 32, v. 33.

" Be still and strong,
O Man, my Brother! hold thy sobbing breath,
And keep thy soul's large window pure from wrong!
That so, as life's appointment issueth,
Thy vision may be clear to watch along
The sunset consummation-lights of death!"

E. B. Browning.

ONE OF the greatest affirmations possible to man is that of the ancient creed, "I believe in the Holy Ghost." All knowledge, power, success, and victory over the world, the flesh, and the devil, depend on the recognition and use of the fellowship or partnership of the Holy Spirit. As Peter said in his great Pentecostal sermon—When our Lord passed through all the Heavens to the right-hand of power, He asked the Father and received from Him the authority, to confer upon each member of His mystical body the infilling and anointing by the Holy Paraclete, as He had Himself received it at His Baptism. As God He was one with the Father and the Holy Spirit; but when He assumed our nature, He was conceived of the Holy Spirit, infilled and anointed by Him, and wrought his life-work in His power and grace. The Father gave not the Holy Spirit by measure to His Son, and it was through the Eternal Spirit that He offered Himself without spot to God.

He ascended that He might receive and bestow gifts on His Church. Of His fulness may all we receive, and grace upon grace. Indeed, unto every one of us grace has been given, according to the measure of the gift of Christ, although we must make the sad confession that we have failed to appropriate our respective shares in the Pentecostal gift. We have been satisfied with half-filled cups, when the river of God might be flowing through our lives. "The promise is to us and to our children, even to as many as the Lord our God shall call"; but how few of us have accepted the enduement, or been anointed by that sacred chrism, with which the Father inaugurated the public ministry of our Saviour, and which He now waits to impart to the humblest and weakest, though they be but as the skirts of His robes.

I. PETER'S PREVIOUS EXPERIENCES.—On the evening of the Resurrection Day the Lord had breathed on him and the rest as they gathered in the Upper Room. "Then said Jesus to them again, Peace be unto you: as My Father hath sent Me, even so send I you. And when He had said this, He breathed on them, and said, 'Receive ye the Holy Spirit.'" We gather, therefore, that their reception of the Spirit was directly intended to qualify them for their mission. It was a distinct equipment for service.

For ten days Peter awaited the promise of the Father, in pursuance of the Master's command: "Tarry ye in the city of Jerusalem, until ye be endued with power from on high."

When the Day of Pentecost was fully come, he, like the rest, was filled by His Advent, and began to speak as the Spirit gave him utterance. Thus we learn that the filling, enduement, and anointing are equivalent terms, and are all associated with the service we are called upon to render. We may have been born of the Spirit, and have so received the seed of the new life, but we must also be anointed by the Spirit, if we expect to be fully used by the Master in our brief mortal life.

When our Apostle faced the Sanhedrim on the morning after the miracle on the cripple at the Beautiful Gate, we are told that on arising to reply to his accusers, he was again suddenly and gloriously filled with the Holy Spirit, proving that we may claim successive and repeated infillings, especially when overtaken by an hour of crisis.

On the return of Peter and John to their own company, the place where they were assembled was shaken as by waves of holy power. They were all filled with the Holy Spirit, and spake the word of God with boldness. "With great power gave the Apostles witness of the Resurrection." Evidently this further experience of the incoming

tides of God fell also to Peter's lot equally with the whole rejoicing
and triumphant company. Why should not we be subject to these
repeated experiences? We have not, because we ask not, and because
we fear to take risks for Jesus Christ!

Peter had also had repeated evidences of the convicting power of
the Spirit of God. "When they heard this, they were pricked in their
heart." Of this quality in the blessed Paraclete we have many conspicuous modern examples. As he was dying, Brainerd said to his
brother: "When ministers feel the special gracious influences of the
Holy Spirit in their hearts, it wonderfully assists them to come at
the consciences of men, and as it were to handle them; whereas
without these, whatever reason or oratory we may employ, we do
but make use of stumps instead of hands." So Peter had discovered.

But further experiences were to be granted before he and his
fellow Apostles fully explored their inheritance as leaders of the
infant Church. They were to be taught that the Divine Spirit had to
do with the collective Church as well as with the individual, and that
He is the President of the Church on earth, the Vicegerent of Christ,
the Supreme Guide and Teacher of His Body, the Co-witness of His
Resurrection, the Superlative Source of Eternal Life.

To adopt the great words of Archer Butler—"When Christ
ascended to the Father He sent forth the Spirit, who should be His
Vicegerent in the Church; and as long as the Sovereign reigns in
Heaven, His Spiritual Viceroy reigns in human souls. They are
correspondent and correlative one to the other. 'If I go not away,'
said the Saviour before He ascended, the Spirit cannot come.' If
He be away, then the Spirit is in the Church. The absence of one is
the presence of the other; or let me rather say that there is no
absence, no presence, no departure, no separation! Christ Himself is
one with the Holy Spirit, and with Him temples in the heart of His
mystical body."

Our Lord may have revealed this great mystery during the forty
days in which He instructed His friends in the things concerning the
Kingdom of God. But their practical realization was gradually
unfolded to Peter and the rest, as Pentecost receded into the back-
ground of their memory. The experience of Peter in this matter is
very illuminating. He was led step by step into the full apprehension
of the Spirit's association with the Church.

II. The Holy Spirit's Presidency of the Church.—It became apparent in connection with the finances of the Church. The multitude of them that believed were of one heart and soul, so that none of them claimed any of his possessions as his own. All was held as a common property. There was therefore no poverty or clamant need. Those who were possessors of lands or houses sold them, and brought the whole amount that had been realized and gave it to the Apostles, by whom distribution was made to every one according to his wants. Out of this fund a certain amount would be laid aside for the rooms and meals which they had in common. So much would be allotted for the maintenance of the Apostles and their fellow-workers. Also the destitute, sickly, and widowed would be relieved according to their requirements. This practice is not to be confused with Communism, because the latter system abolishes all property by force, imposes a compulsory division of profits, and compels all workers to place their possessions and earnings in a common purse. In the early Christian practice, while a field remained unsold, it was still the property of its owners; and when it was sold, the proceeds remained absolutely at their discretion. This system was clearly a temporary expedient for the special circumstances of the Jerusalem Church, and the Apostles made no attempt to institute it in any of the Churches formed among the Gentiles.

Many members of the Church, like the good Barnabas, made great sacrifices, and stood proportionately high in the esteem of their fellow-believers; and their desire to obtain the same notoriety without paying the same price for it led Ananias and his wife to act their lie. They sold some land, and encouraged the belief that they had brought the entire amount obtained for it to place at the Apostles' disposal for the common good. There was no obligation on them to sell the land. There would have been no sin in bringing part of the proceeds, if they had frankly acknowledged that it was only a part. But they pretended that the sum handed to the community was the entire amount of the purchase-money. Thus they gratified their love of money on the one hand and their vanity on the other. It was an acted falsehood.

We will not stay to particularize the duplicates of this sin in modern life. We are all tempted to appropriate credit for more earnestness, prayerfulness, and generosity than we practise. Thank

God, there is no need to yield to this insidious temptation; but who has not been conscious of the suggestion? Thank God, though Satan may flash the suggestion upon our consciousness, the grace of the indwelling Spirit is sufficient to keep it at the threshold, and prevent it from filling the heart. "Why hath Satan *filled* thy heart. . . ." When we are filled with the Spirit, there is no space left for filling by Satan. The air that fills the diving-bell excludes the entrance of the water into which it presently descends. "Walk in the Spirit, and ye shall not fulfil the lusts of the flesh." Ananias and Sapphira did not avail themselves of His grace. They had been enlightened, had welcomed the heavenly gift, had been made partakers of the Holy Spirit, and had tasted the good word of God and the powers of the new era; but they had fallen away, and become as land, which, though it has drunk of the rain that comes off upon it, bears thorns and thistles, and is therefore nigh unto a curse. That curse would never have befallen, if the sin had been confessed, and their crucifying afresh of the Son of God arrested. But in the absence of any sign of compunction in either of them, their sin incurred the punishment of a tragic death. By one stroke they were cut off from membership with the Church, lest the contagion of their sin should spread.

We will now concentrate on Peter's illuminated and illuminating utterances: "Why hath Satan filled thine heart to lie to the Holy Spirit?" . . . "How is it that ye have agreed together to tempt the Spirit of the Lord?" What stronger evidence could be given of the Personality of Deity of the Holy Spirit? It is clearly impossible to tempt or deceive an influence, emanation, or breath. If you lie, you lie to a Person. If you tempt, you tempt a Person. The charge of either implies Personality of the beings concerned, of the Spirit equally as of Ananias or Sapphira. But how was their act a sin against the Spirit of the Lord? Was it not rather committed against that infant society, and notoriously against its poor? Undoubtedly it was a mean-hearted wrong perpetrated on them; but it was so flagrantly a sin against the Spirit that the human aspect sank into comparative insignificance. In point of fact, the Church differs from all other assemblies in this, that it is the Body of Christ and the seat or throne of the Holy Spirit; and this made their sin so flagrant.

If a handful of people, however obscure, gather in the Name of

Christ to consider and further the interests of His Kingdom, the Holy Spirit is not only present, but He presides. He holds court as the Representative and Vicegerent of Christ. He sees to it that in their unanimity after united prayer, the will of Christ is reflected, and that through their united action it is done. What is bound or loosed on earth is in harmony with what is bound and loosed in Heaven.

The Roman Catholic Church makes use of the mysterious word "*See*." It is "the Holy See" from the first syllable of the Latin word *sedere*, to sit, and in reference to the inspired statement that the Holy Spirit on the Day of Pentecost *sat* on each of them. Their inference is that the primitive Church was the seat or throne of the Paraclete, that when Jesus took His seat on the throne at the Father's right hand, the Holy Spirit descended to the throne of the Church, and that the Apostate Church of the Seven Hills is the lineal descendant of that Church. We are prepared to accept the two first of these propositions, but not the last. It is quite true that when our Lord went up to His throne in the Heavens, the Holy Spirit came down to His in the Church. It is quite true that the Church is the throne from which the Divine Spirit issues His mandates, and through which He exerts His energy. But it is not true that Rome is that throne or seat Nay, verily, but wherever a group of people meet in the Name of Jesus, and for the maintenance of the holy ordinances which He enjoined, and uniting for mutual edification and for the purposes of His Kingdom, *there* you have the divine seat and throne, and *there* you may count on the living Presence of the Sevenfold Spirit of the Eternal. "Grace to you and Peace from the Seven Spirits which are before His throne and from Jesus Christ." Happy is that Christian community which understands and realizes this blessed fact, as it was perceived and realized by Peter and the rest on that momentous day, when the Serpent threatened to enter their newly-planted Paradise, as he entered and destroyed the Paradise of Eden.

The falsehood on which these two sinners against their own souls agreed was sin against God the Holy Spirit, and through Him against the Lord Jesus; and the penalty which was inflicted was due to his own direct action, as a warning for all after-time. "And great fear came upon the whole Church and upon all those that heard these things." Would that similar fear, the fear born of reverent love, might come upon all gatherings of God's people! There would be more intensity in every act of worship, more love and faith, more of the adoration and humility which are evident in that upper sanctuary, where the very seraphim veil their faces with their wings as they hymn the praise of the All-Holy. Keep thy foot, when thou enterest the House of God, if the Church is in session, for God is there by His Spirit. Worship Him in spirit and truth! Refuse to harbour anything which is not consistent with His Nature! And bring with thee in thine own ardent heart some contribution to the solemn and blessed atmosphere, in which He expands His tenderest and mightiest energies. Thus when we meet with the Church, let us do so under the searching gaze of its President, and in Him draw nigh to the General Assembly and Church of the firstborn, whose names are written in Heaven, to the spirits of just men made perfect, to God the Judge of all, and to Jesus the Mediator of the new Covenant.

III. THE CO-WITNESS OF THE HOLY SPIRIT.—The public sentiment of Jerusalem was strongly in favour of the Church. This was largely accounted for by miraculous works of healing that gathered the crowds around the Apostles, as formerly to the Person of the Lord. In the early days of His popularity the people pressed to touch Him. "Wheresoever He entered, into villages, or into cities, or into the country, they laid the sick in the market-places, and besought that they might touch if it were but the border of His garment; and as many as touched Him were made whole." Those scenes were repeated in the narrow streets of Jerusalem, that as Peter came by his shadow might be cast at least on some of the sick who were laid on beds and couches along his pathway. The tidings of the marvellous cures which were effected spread to the cities and towns round about and attracted immense multitudes to see and hear and be healed. The country rang with the tidings of the wondrous cures wrought in the Name of Jesus.

For a time the Rulers stood rigidly aloof. "Of the rest," i.e., of those who were not of the ranks of the common people, "durst not man join himself to them." But finally the smouldering embers of their jealousy burst into fire, and the whole Apostolic band was arrested and thrust into the public prison. On the following morning, when the Sanhedrim, reinforced by others of the elders, or senate of Israel, met to adjudge the matter, the prison was empty, and news came that their prisoners were standing in the Temple and teaching the people. Notwithstanding the miraculous character of their liberation, the trial was proceeded with, and Peter, as spokesman of the whole body, had another opportunity of proclaiming before the ruling classes of the nation the Resurrection and Exaltation of his Lord.

That the God of their fathers had raised up Jesus whom they slew; that He was seated at His right hand; that He was Prince and Saviour; that repentance and remission of sin were offered through Him to Israel—these truths had been voiced in that august assembly before; but there was a new emphasis laid on the corroborating witness of the Holy Spirit. "We are witnesses of these things; and so is the Holy Spirit whom God hath given to them that obey Him."

The Master had promised that this should be their experience. "When the Comforter is come, whom I will send unto you from the Father, even the Spirit of Truth which proceedeth from the Father, He shall bear witness of Me; and ye also shall bear witness, because ye have been with Me from the beginning." There we have the Saviour's own promise that the Church may count on the corroborating affirmations of the Spirit of Truth. When the voice is heard from Heaven, proclaiming the blessedness of those that have died in Christ, the Spirit utters His emphatic *Amen* in the hearts of men. In the story of Paul's first missionary campaign we are told that the Lord bare witness to the word of His grace; and in the opening chapters of the Epistle to the Hebrews we learn that God bare witness to the earliest Evangelists of the Cross by signs, and wonders, and gifts of the Holy Spirit. Always the Spirit and the Bride say, Come. The Bride says it audibly, "Come, Lord Jesus, come quickly." The Spirit confirms her words with groanings that cannot be uttered, though they pervade the soul.

It was a great discovery and announcement that Peter made that day. It is of immense and transcendent importance to us all! Often when the preacher or teacher is most appalled with the obstinacy and resistance of the human heart, he may comfort himself by remembering that he is in partnership with the Divine. The child's finger may be able only to strike one note after another with one finger on the piano keys, but who will break his heart over such a trifle, when a master of music sits beside her accompanying each of her notes with magnificent thrilling chords, and is able to turn even her mistakes into profounder harmonies? We must never allow that thought of the co-witness of the Divine Spirit on the behalf of the truth to fade from our minds. Obviously we must see to it that we utter only such truths as He will find it possible to corroborate. As Peter put it in this address, it is when we announce Jesus as dying, rising, and exalted, as Saviour and Prince, as the Fountain and Lord of Life, that we may count most surely on the Divine Spirit endorsing and attesting the truth, as though He said: "It is so! By Me He offered Himself without spot to God. I was there when He died. His blood atones. I am One with Him, in the stream which proceeds from the throne of the Lamb. We are One both in its current and its source."

IV. THE SUPERLATIVE SUPERIORITY OF THE HOLY SPIRIT.—The Evangelist Philip had been the means of a marvellous spiritual revival at Samaria, and had there encountered in Simon a crafty and ambitious man, who was clearly an adept in the occult learning of the age and in the black arts of sorcery and witch-craft. Miracles were wrought by his collusion with demon influences, which in our own time have revived under the name of Spiritualism. This science has been defined as an attempt to obtain power by the aid of unknown and spiritual agencies, without regard to those moral and religious conditions of purity and piety under which alone will God discover Himself to man. As in Egypt Jannes and Jambres withstood Moses, so did Simon endeavour to counterfeit the beneficent achievements of Philip, using only the Name of Jesus. Forthwith unclean spirits surrendered their victims with loud cries, and many that were palsied and lame were healed. But the Evangelist was not content with these manifestations of spiritual power, he preached unto them the Christ, and the people gave heed with one accord and believed. "There was great joy in that city!"

Presently a demand arose for further help than Philip could give, and the Apostles, who had remained in Jerusalem, notwithstanding the persecution, which broke out after Stephen's death, that they might focus and guide the entire Christian movement, sent Peter and John to give on their behalf formal recognition to the infant Christian Church which had arisen from the gracious work of this Revival. During the solemn act which sought and obtained a further bestowal of the Holy Spirit, there seems to have been such a conspicuous manifestation of spiritual power as astounded the beholders and specially Simon. With amazement he beheld the exaltation that transfigured spirit, soul and body, and lifted the converts into unparalleled ecstasy. If only he could obtain the talisman of a similar power it would be worth a mine of gold; and so he hazarded the offer which has for ever stamped his name with the infamy, and made it, as Simony, the brand of similar proposals. Turning on the wretched and misguided man, Peter sternly rebuked him. "Thy silver perish with thee, because thou hast thought that the Gift of God may be obtained by money. Thou hast neither part nor lot in this matter; for thy heart is not right with God." But, as Peter uttered those terrible words, did there not break in on his soul, by force of contrast, a fresh and living conception, not only of the superlative power of the Holy Spirit, but of the divine purity and beauty of His workmanship, and of the absolute necessity that the character of those with whom He co-operates must also be pure and holy, free from the taint of greed, and able to receive His blessed help, with no selfish ambition, but as the humble and cleansed channels and instruments of His will? "Be ye clean that bear the vessels of the Lord!"

The lesson of Uzzah in the Old Testament and of Ananias in the New compels one to self-examination lest we too may sin against the awful holiness of God. If His nature is Love, and comparable to fire, we must remember that fire consumes. Especially in prayer, though we know that He is our Father, let us ask for grace that we may offer acceptable service, with reverence and awe. "Take off the shoes from off thy feet, for the place whereon thou standest is Holy Ground!"

XXI

THE DOOR OF FAITH UNTO THE GENTILES

ACTS vi. 1–7, viii. 14–25, ix. 31, x. 16.

" *While ye sit idle, do you think*
  The Lord's great work sits idle too?
  That light dare not o'erleap the brink
  Of morn, because 'tis dark with you?
  Though yet your valleys skulk in night
  In God's ripe fields the day is cried,
  And reapers with their sickles bright
  Troop, singing, down the mountain-side."

Lowell.

WE OPEN at this point a new chapter in the history of the unfolding of the Divine purpose for our race. Let us take the shoes from off our feet, for this surely is holy ground. "O the depth of the riches, both of the wisdom and the knowledge of God. Who hath known the mind of the Lord? or who hath been His counsellor. For of Him, and through Him, and to Him are all things."

There are certain facts which we must recapitulate as we seek to understand the mystery or secret, which in other generations was not made known unto the sons of men, as it has now been revealed by the Divine Spirit, who searcheth all things, yea, the deep things of God.

We agree that the Church was born on the day of our Lord's Resurrection. He had always referred to it in the future tense. "I *will* build my Church." When He descended, to use the Apostle's words, "into the lower parts of the earth," He laid the foundations on which the glorious edifice arose which was to be builded together —a house not made by hands—as a habitation of God by the Spirit.

We agree that when the Saviour ascended to His throne in the Heavens, the Divine Comforter, as His Executor, descended to His throne or seat in the Church, to become its Teacher, Inspirer, and Guide. "He *sat* upon each of them." God is still resident among men. As the Lord Jesus was incarnated in "that holy thing" which was born of the Virgin, so the Holy Spirit became incarnated in the Church, which is His Body, the fulness of Him that filleth all in all.

We agree also that from the first the Divine objective was to include in the one Church, not Jews alone, but Gentiles who had not received the seal and sign of the Abrahamic covenant, but had entered directly from the Gentile world by the simple act of faith. This was God's secret purpose, as Paul tells us in the closing paragraph of his Epistle to the Romans, which had been hidden from before times eternal, and the unfolding of which was especially entrusted to him, as to one born out of due time, but specially honoured to be the Apostle of the Gentiles. Until the reception of Cornelius into the Church, the idea had hardly dawned on the Apostles or the body of disciples that the Gentiles should be fellow-heirs, and fellow-members of the body, and fellow-partakers of the promise of Christ. Gentiles, it was generally supposed, could only enter the door of the Christian Church by first becoming Jews. The Scripture indeed foresaw that God would justify the Gentiles *by faith*, and by faith alone. This Gospel was preached beforehand unto Abraham, in the earliest stages of his career as the father of them that believe; and he is not a Jew which is one outwardly, but he is a Jew which is one inwardly, and circumcision is that of the heart, in the spirit, and not in the letter, whose praise is not of men, but of God. When our Lord commissioned His Apostles to go into all the world and make disciples from all the nations, they probably supposed that the rite of circumcision would precede their administration of baptism. It was only by a very gradual process that the whole truth broke on them that in Christ Jesus there is neither Jew nor Greek, circumcision nor uncircumcision, bond nor free, male nor female, but all are one in Him.

We agree that it was befitting that he, to whom the keys of the Kingdom were committed, and who had opened the door of Pentecostal blessing to Jews, should be honoured by fulfilling the same ministry to the Gentiles also. For eight years with his fellow Apostles Peter had confined himself to the consolidation of the Mother Church, he was now to learn that her children would be gathered

equally from a great multitude, whom none could number, of every
nation, and kindred, and people, and tongue. We have, therefore, to
consider the steps by which he was led forth into a larger conception
of the Divine purpose, by that guiding cloud, which led him out of
the Jerusalem of bondage to an outward ordinance into the Jerusalem
that is above, which is eternally and spiritually free.

Peter was a strict Jew. He was inclined to view with suspicion
even the Hellenist, or Greek-speaking, Jews, who were scattered
throughout the Roman Empire. And he knew the Gentiles, only as
he had, from boyhood, beheld the glitter of their civilization, which
transformed the Lake of Galilee into a Roman pleasure-resort. He
was intimately acquainted with Roman officials, collectors of revenue,
centurions and soldiers; but he had never entered a Gentile home,
had never sat at a Gentile table, and had never transgressed the rigid
prescriptions of the Levitical dietary. He shrank from familiar intercourse with Gentiles, as a Brahmin in India to-day with a Sudra.
Hence his exclamation, when invited to eat of the heterogeneous
contents of the great sheet: "Not so, Lord, for I have never eaten
anything that was common or unclean."

The Divine Master is willing to take infinite pains with us, before
He demands the ceding of our wills and the taking of an irrevocable
step. He causes the light of His illuminating Spirit to fall on us,
before calling us to strike our tents for a march into the unknown.
The reasonableness, necessity, and urgency of some course to which
we are summoned, are unfolded, "line upon line, precept upon
precept, here a little and there a little, by divers portions and in
divers manners."

Let us watch the stages of the process in the present case.

(1) *There arose a murmuring of the Grecian, the Hellenist, Jews
against the Hebrews.* The Hellenist always regarded Jerusalem and
the Temple with fond and reverent affection. Thither he turned as
he prayed. Thither he came with his family, as often as the cost
permitted, to the annual festivals. In the Holy City he desired to die,
and in its precincts be buried. A large contingent of these Jews of the
dispersion were present on the Day of Pentecost, and had then, as
in the following years, identified themselves with the Christian
community. Many of them, like the good Barnabas, had parted with
their possessions, placing the proceeds in the common stock, and

their poor were in the habit of receiving their sustenance from the common purse. But suddenly the calm waters of Peace and Love became ruffled by dissatisfaction and heart-burning. Their widows complained that undue partiality was shown in the daily distribution, and that home-born women fared better at the hand of the Apostolic almoners than they did.

The peril of a serious rent in the seamless robe of the Church became at length so imminent that Peter and his brethren were compelled to take action. After anxious consideration, they arrived at the conclusion that their highest vocation was to prayer and the ministry of the Word, and that this service of tables should be entrusted to seven men of good report, full of the Holy Spirit and wisdom. They advised the Church, therefore, as the ultimate authority, that they should proceed to choose that number from amongst themselves. "Look ye out therefore, brethren, from among you seven men, whom we may appoint over this business, but we will continue steadfastly in prayer and in the ministry of the Word."

In a parenthesis we may notice the importance of this action, and the light it casts on the precise position that Peter occupied in the primitive Church. If he had been invested with the authority which has been attributed to him by those who have specially posed as his successors, it is inconceivable that he should have left this momentous decision to the general assembly of believers. Surely he would have acted on his own authority, and with the acquiescence of his fellow Apostles would have appointed these seven deacons. But it was not so. The Church must elect, and the Apostles, by prayer and the laying on of hands, endorse their choice.

It is remarkable that they were all Hellenist Jews, with the exception of the last, who was a Gentile proselyte. The unanimity of the Church in this solemn act was so evidently due to the presence and direction of the Spirit, whose supreme action had been apparent in the case of Ananias and his wife, that Peter could say nothing to the contrary, however startling to his preconceptions such action must have appeared.

(2) *Then came the great arguments, apology, and martyrdom of Stephen.* In the familiar intercourse that ensued, Peter would have been attracted to the eloquent young Hellenist, whose face must

often have shone "as the face of an angel." He often listened to the
burning words with which Stephen insisted that throughout their
history the chosen people had resisted the Divine Spirit, when He
summoned them to a new advance. The note of a trumpet-call rang
through his speech in private conference and public debate. And,
as he listened, Peter may have recalled the Master's words, that it
would be found impossible to put the new wine in the old bottles.
Almost unconsciously his mind must have been prepared for a more
generous interpretation of his Master's purpose. Already the breath
of a new age fanned his cheek, as the door was being slowly opened
for the admission of the Gentile world.

(3) *The mission to Samaria followed.* Beneath Philip's preaching
vast numbers of Samaritans, who had for long been held under the
spell of what we now know as Spiritualism, had broken away from
Simon the Sorcerer, and been baptized in the name of Jesus. This
movement needed to be regularized, and the Apostles, who had
dared to remain in Jerusalem, despite Saul's fiery persecution,
determined to commission Peter and John to visit the scene of
revival, and lead the new converts forward into the full enjoyment of
the gifts of Pentecost. The heart of the Church was still beating
strongly, though so many of its sons and daughters had been obliged
to flee for their lives.

Here, again, Peter used the keys of teaching, prayer, and the
imposition of hands, with the result that the miracle of Pentecost was
repeated. "They received the Holy Ghost." Though the special
rite of the Abrahamic covenant was of national observance among
the Samaritans, they were regarded as a mongrel race. Their name
was employed as a term of reproach. "Thou art a Samaritan!" A
good deed like that attributed to the Good Samaritan was not
generally expected from a race that was looked upon as accursed.
But, to the obvious astonishment of the Apostles, the Holy Spirit,
in answer to their prayer, descended on these believing Samaritans,
with absolute impartiality. Indeed, Peter was so impressed with
what he saw that he could do no other than keep in the current of
the Divine purpose; and therefore he and John, in their leisurely
return to Jerusalem, preached in the villages of Samaria through
which they passed. Here, again, was a further unfolding of the
horizon of God's purpose.

(4) *But the process was still further accelerated by the conversion of Saul of Tarsus.* It was a startling rumour that reached Jerusalem, that the arch-persecutor of the Church had been arrested by the direct intervention of the Lord, and had become His humble follower. But as the further tidings filtered in, and fuller details were furnished of this wonderful event, they learnt that Saul had been compelled to flee from Damascus and had gone to Arabia. Some time elapsed, and finally, to Peter's surprise, he presented himself at his humble dwelling in Jerusalem, and took up his abode there, remaining as his guest for fifteen days. We are strongly tempted to draw aside the veil and consider the converse of these two men, so different in age, education, and mental outlook, and yet so closely united in Jesus Christ. Did not the newly-constituted Apostle, who had just seen the Risen Lord, ask his new-found friend to take him through the scenes associated with the Master's closing days? Would they not go together outside the city wall to Gethsemane, Calvary, and Joseph's Garden? "There He lay on that plot of grass, and I came thereafterwards at dawn, when my heart was breaking." "It was on this spot that I drew my sword, because I couldn't endure to see them binding His dear hands so roughly." "Yes, we will go to Calvary." "That's where His cross was lifted up, I could just catch the outline, as I stood in the distance, but it was very dark." "I couldn't stay to the end, because the mother was in an agony, and one of us had to be with her; so I went back to release John, who was staying with her till I returned." "Now come to the grave." "They laid Him there on the Friday afternoon, but at daybreak, on the first day of the week, the women brought a message that He was alive and wanted to see me." "In that glade yonder we met, but I can never tell all that happened there. It is locked up in His heart and mine." Thus Peter must have told the story, whilst Paul listened with rapt interest.

Thus the fortnight passed, when suddenly the younger man burst in on Peter with a strange glory on his features, as though he had seen, as Isaiah did, the Lord high and lifted up, his train filling the Temple, whilst the seraphim, in a burning row, stood around with their ceaseless ascription of holiness. "Brother," said he, "what do you think, as just now I was praying in the Temple I seemed to lose myself, and saw the Lord, and He said to me, Make haste, and get thee quickly out of Jerusalem, because they will not receive of thee testimony concerning Me. And I said, Lord, they know that I imprisoned and beat in every synagogue them that believed on Thee. But He said unto me, Depart: for I will send thee forth far hence to the Gentiles. You see, therefore, I have no alternative, and must be gone."

Peter must have been sorely troubled at the danger which beset his new-found friend, and took instant steps to arrange his passage out of the danger-zone for Cæsarea, and ultimately to Tarsus. When he was safely away, however, those parting words must have rung in his heart—Far hence to the Gentiles. He could not challenge those words. Clearly they were spoken by the Master, but they still further prepared him for the fresh demand which would soon be made on himself.

(5) *The process was completed at Joppa.* After the departure of Paul the Church throughout Judæa and Samaria had peace, and walking in the Paracletism of the Paraclete was multiplied. Peter took advantage of this halcyon period to make an itinerary through the smaller congregations that were scattered throughout Judæa, and in course of time came to Lydda, where, as the medium for the health-giving word of Christ, he lifted Æneas from his eight-years' paralysis. Thence he was summoned by an urgent message to Joppa, six and a half miles distant on the rocky seacoast, to the room of death, where the beloved Dorcas lay. His prayer on her behalf prevailed with God, and when he gave her his hand she arose to become once more the gentle friend of all the saints and widows in the little town.

There, however, his work seemed finished. Before him lay the sea of the Gentiles. Its restless waters were the symbol of the restless fret of a world without Christ, and at the end of its resources. The house in which he lodged—the house of Simon the tanner—had associations with death and its accompanying ceremonial pollution, which must have been extremely distasteful to a conscientious Jew. The Jerusalem Church had become so diminished by persecution, and flight, that its concerns failed to afford him the wide scope and sphere to which for eight years he had been accustomed. What was to be the next step in the fulfilment of his life-work? Was the cloud about to move forward? Was some new development of the Divine pattern at hand which he must realize for himself and others?

At this juncture, one noon, when the blazing sunshine poured down on the burnished mirror of the sea, and on the white houses of the little town, he went up to the housetop for prayer—prayer probably for further light. Whilst they prepared the midday meal, he fell into a trance, and through the opened heavens he caught the vision of a redeemed world, like a great white sheet. The variety of its contents—four-footed beasts, creeping things, birds clean and unclean, startled him; and still more the declaration that God had cleansed them all, that the old Levitical restrictions were removed, and that any of them were fit for food. Rise, Peter, slay and eat.

Then, whilst he was much perplexed in himself as to what the vision which he had seen might mean, the knocking at the gate, the voices of men, that rose in the noon-silence, as they called his name, together with the assurance of the Spirit that there was no need for fear or hesitation—all indicated that the hour of Destiny had struck, that a new epoch was inaugurated, and that he was to lead the Church into the greatest revolution she had known since the Ascension of her Lord.

What a lesson is here for our perplexed and anxious hearts! We find it so difficult to wait the Lord's leisure. Like imprisoned birds we beat our breasts against the wires of the cage. Though we pray, we do not trust. We find it so hard to obey the injunction of the Psalmist and roll our care, our way, and ourselves on God. Let us be silent to Him, and believe that even now the messengers are hastening along the road, with the summons, or direction, or help we need. "I will stand upon my watch, and set me upon the tower, and will look forth to see what He will speak. The vision is yet for the appointed time, and it panteth towards the end. Though it tarry, wait for it, because it will surely come. The just shall live by his faith."

XXII

THE BREAKING OF THE YOKE

ACTS x. 17, xi. 18.

"Yet he who at the sixth hour sought
The lone house-top to pray,
There gained a sight beyond his thought—
The dawn of Gentile day.
Then reckon not, when perils lour,
The time of prayer mis-spent;
Nor meanest chance, nor place, nor hour
Without its heavenward bent."

Newman.

WITHOUT doubt the Levitical system, in its strict prohibition of certain kinds of food, as set forth in Lev. xi., placed a very heavy yoke on the neck of the Hebrew people. In fact, at the first General Council of the Church Peter described it as a yoke, "which neither they nor their fathers had been able to bear." It was obviously intended to secure their separateness from all other nations, so that they might become a peculiar treasure, a Kingdom of priests, and a holy nation, specially set apart for the Divine use. A middle wall of partition was erected between Jew and Gentile, that nothing might dilute or impair the sacred deposit of truth committed to Abraham and his seed. But hard as the restrictions were, there was no hesitation in their maintenance. In the fiery persecution of the Jews by Antiochus, men chose rather to die than defile themselves with meats, and so profane the holy covenant. The refusal to eat swine's flesh was ranked with circumcision and Sabbath-observance as a matter for which a Jew should unhesitatingly lay down his life.

As the result of these food-prescriptions, the Gentile world was viewed as strangers and foreigners, "far off," aliens from the

159

commonwealth of Israel, and strangers to the covenants of promise. They were without God and without hope. If they desired to be received into the Palace of the Great King, they must travel round by the tents of Abraham and the wilderness of Sinai. It was consonant with this that certain men came down from the Mother Church to the earliest Church formed exclusively of Gentiles, saying —"Except ye be circumcised after the manner of Moses, ye cannot be saved."

It was clearly necessary that the cancelling of Levitical distinctions should be as clearly defined as their imposition; and therefore Peter's Vision, the embassy from Cornelius, and the manifest corroboration by the Holy Spirit were concentrated in this remarkable episode. Peter and Cornelius were brought together, and so was opened the new and living way which the Lord had already consecrated through His flesh. We Gentiles have been made nigh by the blood of Christ, because He hath reconciled us to God in one body by the Cross.

The Unveiling of the Mystery took three days.

I. CAESAREA: 3.0 P.M.—Cornelius came of one of the noblest of Roman families. He belonged to the same stock as the Scipios, Sulla, and the mother of the Gracchi. "No name was more honourable at Rome than that of the *Cornelian House.* An earnest seeker after God, he had grown weary of the polytheism, idolatry, and superstitions of his age, and had sought satisfaction in the one faith that presented the conception of the Unity and Spirituality of God, together with a strenuous demand for purity, righteousness, and mercy. Amid widespread atheism, the ceaseless conflict of rival schools, and the foul corruption of morals, the severe ideals of the Hebrew Scriptures stood as a white sunlit peak shooting up amid the profound shadows of departing night; and large numbers of the heathen world were attracted. "Behold darkness shall cover the earth and gross darkness the peoples: but the Lord shall arise upon thee, and His glory shall be seen upon thee; and nations shall come to thy light, and kings to the brightness of thy rising."

When Cornelius took up his quarters in the splendid city which Herod had created, some thirty miles to the north of Joppa, he was brought into yet closer contact with the religion and literature of the

Old Testament. As he studied them he became increasingly impressed, and there grew up within his soul an earnest desire for those fuller revelations of the Divine, to which seers and prophets, priests and kings had incessantly borne witness. He was a devout man, generous in his gifts to the poor, careful to maintain religion with all his household, and constant in prayer. His domestics and his orderly regarded him as "a just man," and he was "of good report among the Jews." Probably he was a proselyte of the Gate, and carefully observed the prescribed hours of daily prayer. But with all this he was not satisfied, and at that time was apparently passing through a deep exercise of soul. He was seeking goodly pearls, but had not found the one Pearl of great price, to obtain which he would have been well satisfied to part with all.

He knew that he was ostracized by the Jews—was it his duty to submit to their initial rite and be received into their synagogue as one of themselves? He had heard of Jesus of Nazareth, His holy life, His miracles, His teaching—would it be wise to enrol himself with His followers? Not improbably it was in connection with these and kindred problems that he set apart one quiet day to ascertain by prayer and fasting what God's will might be. He had offered many previous prayers of the same kind: "Thy *prayers* and thine alms are gone up for a memorial before God." But this prayer was more specific and urgent: "Cornelius, thy *prayer* is heard." He had reached such a pitch of intensity that his soul was dissolved in one passionate cry for help. "I . . . prayer," said the Psalmist. "I will not let Thee go unless Thou bless me! Tell me, I pray Thee, Thy name. And He blessed him there."

> *Wrestling I will not let Thee go,*
> *Till I Thy name and nature know.*

Suddenly an angel stood beside him. His messengers, in recounting the incident to Peter, described him as "a holy angel." Cornelius himself spoke of him as "a man in bright apparel." The Lord is good to them that wait for Him, to the soul that seeketh Him. He will fulfil the desire of them that fear Him. He that willeth to do His will shall know. Let us follow on to know the Lord; His going forth is sure as the morning. At first, brave soldier as he was, and accustomed to face danger, Cornelius was greatly startled by this sudden contact with the spirit-world. Recovering himself, he asked: "What is it, Lord?" and was told that his prayer for light and guidance would be answered through the instrumentality of one Simon, surnamed Peter, who was lodging at a tanner's house in Joppa, abutting on the shore.

It is well worth our notice that God does not commission Angels to evangelize the world or instruct His saints in the mysteries of the Kingdom. There is a sense in which He taketh not hold of Angels, but of the sons of men. On each Lord's Day He might have opened the gates of Heaven and sent bands of Angels to instruct and inspire us; but it is not so. The treasure is placed in earthen vessels. Men and women, full of human sin and frailty, are chosen as His ambassadors to their fellows. "Moreover He said to me, Son of man, all My words that I shall speak unto thee receive in thine heart, and hear with thine ears; and get thee to the children of thy people and speak unto them." The Angel could have spoken almost all Peter's sermon and more, but all that he was sent to do was to tell Cornelius to send for the fisherman—Apostle. Not for Philip the evangelist, though he was residing in the same city, because he had not passed through the same exercises of soul or had reached the same point of vision as Peter. Let us never forget that the soul-discipline through which we may be passing is carefully designed to make us meet for the Master's use, and to prepare us to deliver a definite message with the profound sympathy and understanding of personal experience. "What I tell you in darkness, that speak ye in light, and what ye hear in the ear, that proclaim ye upon the housetops." God always knows where to find His chosen instruments. Their addresses are registered in Heaven.

II. JOPPA: 12.0 NOON.—Cornelius lost no time in acting on the vision. As soon as the Angel had stepped back behind the curtain of sense, he called for, and despatched to Joppa, two household servants and a devout soldier, all of whom sympathized with his religious convictions. They were able to cover part of the distance during the remaining hours of the afternoon, and finished their journey at noon on the following day.

Peter, as we have seen, was just emerging from an ecstasy in which he beheld the vision of a redeemed world, and God had showed him that he should not call any man common or unclean. He naturally realized that ·if the distinction between clean and unclean animals was abolished, the abolition of the distinction between Hebrew and Gentile was necessarily implied. The middle partition wall had been demolished. The grace of God had overflowed the dams and banks by which it had been restrained. Salvation was as impartial as the dew or rain, which knows no delimitation of frontier, but refreshes with equal love the adjacent fields of just and unjust, bond and free, Samaritan, Gentile and Jew.

In personal experience, before we step out on an unknown path, let us wait for our visions to be corroborated by the knocking at the door and the clear bidding of the Spirit. Peter was encouraged and assured by the concurrence of these three. "While Peter thought on the *vision*, the *Spirit* said unto him, 'Behold, *three men* seek thee.'" In connection with this conjunction we must never lose sight of the urgent need of uniting Visions and Duties. We are always standing between the two. Each of us has visions, clearer or duller, in sunlight or starlight, bright and beautiful, or clouded and obscure; and each is beset with the knock and appeal of our fellows: from the sharp knock of the telegram to the soft tap of feeble age or tiny childhood Not the vision without the task, or we become dreamers and visionaries. Not the task without the vision, or we become as dumb driven cattle. When you are doubtful whether your vision is from God, wait for the further indication of His will through circumstance. Listen for the three men knocking and calling in the street beneath. And when you have been assured to this extent, wait for the still small voice of the Holy Spirit, saying, "Arise, and get thee down, and go with them, nothing doubting, for I have sent them."

All Peter's doubts vanished. His hesitation was ended. He invited the three men into the house, shared with them the meal which had been preparing, lodged them for the night, and on the following morning started with them on the journey to Cæsarea. They must have travelled by the great high road which skirted the shore of the Mediterranean. During the afternoon, whilst the messengers were resting, Peter had secured the companionship of six believing Jews, under the evident impression that he was taking a step which would be closely scrutinized by the Apostles and leaders at Jerusalem. The journey of these ten men occupied more than a day, and it was on the morning of the third day from Peter's vision that the party entered Cæsarea—the city of marble palaces, and seat of Roman Government. How incredulous the citizens would have been if they had been informed that in the coming time the chief interest taken in their proud city would arise from its association with that group of travel-worn pedestrians, who one morning in A.D. 43 or 44 passed through the city gates, and wended their way to the Roman barracks, to have an interview with the officer in command. Only a few ruins attest the site of Herod's city, whereas the visit of Peter and his companions dated the beginning of a movement which has affected the entire world.

CÆSAREA: 3.0 P.M.—Cornelius seems to have been the centre of a religious circle of relatives and near friends, whom he had informed of his recent experiences, and had invited to share with him the help of which the Angel had given the assurance. The time for the return of his messengers, with their expected guest, had been carefully calculated, and at the appointed hour many came together. In the words of the host, they were all present in the sight of God to hear the things with which the Lord had entrusted His servant on their behalf.

When it was announced that the party had arrived, Cornelius met them at the outer gate, and with instinctive reverence and courtesy prostrated himself before the man who had been commissioned by a message from the Unseen. Peter instantly stooped to raise him, saying, "Stand up; I myself also am a man." Well would it have been if all his successors had imitated his manly simplicity and humility. As they passed together to the assembly-room, where the expectant gathering awaited them, he spoke so pleasantly and familiarly that his host was placed entirely at his ease, and he was able to detail the marvellous circumstances which had led to the present meeting. At the close of his brief address he added, "Thou hast done well that thou art come"—a sentiment in which many around him shared. Then, amid the awed hush, in an atmosphere charged with spiritual emotion, and with the consciousness that he was in the current of the Divine purpose, Peter opened his mouth and spoke.

His address fell into three distinct compartments. He told again the well-known story of Jesus, who, though habited in the guise of great humility, was nevertheless Lord of all. He gave his emphatic personal testimony to His Resurrection from the grave—"We ate and drank with Him after He rose from the dead." Finally he proclaimed the forgiveness and remission of sin through faith in His Name. Not a word was uttered about circumcision. There was no suggestion that they must pass through the synagogue to the Church. Neither Abraham nor Moses was mentioned. The one condition of forgiveness was faith in Him, whom the Jews slew, hanging Him on a tree, but whom God raised from the dead. The offer was made to men of every nation, wherever they feared God and wrought righteousness; whether Jew or Gentile, they were welcome to close with God's great offer of forgiveness and peace, and would be "accepted in the Beloved."

No burst of eloquence or charm of speech adorned this simple address. Indeed, Peter had only begun to speak when an indescribable impression swept over the audience, as the summer breeze breathes over the rustling corn. It was as though the Spirit of God were eager to get at once to work, and put Peter gently aside. On the Day of Pentecost the Apostle had time to develop his argument and drive home his appeal; but in this case neither the one nor the other was required. The Holy Spirit fell on all them which heard the word. There was no startling sound from Heaven, and no lambent flame, but there was the gift of tongues. And the six brethren who had accompanied Peter were amazed as they heard them speaking with tongues and magnifying God.

Whilst Peter witnessed that scene, as he said afterwards, it reminded him of Pentecost. "As I began to speak the Holy Spirit fell on them, even as on us at the beginning; and I remembered the word of the Lord how He said, John indeed baptized with water, but ye shall be baptized with the Holy Spirit. God gave unto them the like gift as He did also unto us, when we believed on the Lord Jesus Christ." There were the same upturned gaze, the same enraptured look into the face of Jesus, the same desire to speak of His beauty, the same consciousness of supernatural power. The whole company, which before had been a group of separate units, were suddenly welded into a Unity and became a Church.

Is not this scene full of encouragement? There is doubtless a sense in which the Advent of the Holy Spirit, first to the Jews on the Day of Pentecost, and secondly to the Gentiles in the house of Cornelius, can be no more repeated than the birth and nativity of our Lord; but there is another sense in which each Gentile soul may experience the same Divine infilling. Through Christ Jesus the blessing of Abraham has come upon the Gentiles so "that we may receive the promise of the Spirit by faith." As by faith we receive the saving grace of Jesus, so by faith we may receive the filling, and the repeated fillings, of the Holy Spirit. But such faith always exists in union with an entire surrender of the will, and devout fellowship with God through Scripture. Why should not each reader study once more Gal. iii., and at verse 14 claim his inheritance? Are we not joint-heirs with Christ? There may be no emotional response, but the reckoning of faith cannot be ashamed. Would that every minister and teacher were so filled, that the Holy Spirit might fall, as soon as we commenced to speak. It was said of Finney that on one occasion, when passing through a factory, a girl made an approbrious remark about him, which he overheard. He turned to look at her, and instantly she cried out under a deep conviction of sin, which so spread among the workpeople, that the whole place became a Bochim of tears and prayers. *Forasmuch as God gave unto them the like gift which He did unto us.* Have we received that same gift? There are five tests which supply an infallible answer. If so:

1. The Lord Jesus will be an abiding presence in our lives.
2. The Prayer-life will become increasingly real.
3. The Self-life will be kept on the Cross.
4. There will be unmistakable but quiet power in service.
5. The Spirit of Grace and Love will be conspicuously present in our behaviour and conversation. Have we received? If not, why not? "Let him that is athirst take of the river of life freely." It flows from the throne of God and of the Lamb.

In the case of Cornelius and his friends, the Baptism by the Spirit was immediately followed by baptism in water. The inward grace was ratified by the outward act. Following the rule which Paul observed afterwards, Peter did not himself baptize, probably to guard against the impression that the ordinance derived special sanctity from the person who administered it. He left it therefore to the six brethren from Joppa to complete the formal acceptance of these Gentile disciples into the Christian Church. Cæsarea to-day, but Rome presently!

IV. THE CHALLENGE OF THE MOTHER CHURCH.—The tidings of what Peter had done soon reached Jerusalem, and he lost no time in returning to give in his personal impression and reports. Not Jerusalem only, but the brethren throughout Judæa had heard that the Gentiles also had received the Word of God, from which we may infer that the news had occasioned vast excitement and probably misunderstanding. The circumstances which had led the leader of the Church to make so serious an innovation on recognized custom and procedure required careful consideration before they could recognize his act or welcome the new converts. The Evangelist tells us that when Peter was come up to Jerusalem, "they that were of the circumcision" contended with him. From this we gather that within the Church there was already forming a strong conservative party, which afterwards gave much trouble, and insisted with obstinate tenacity that the Gentile must submit to the Jewish rite before admission to their ranks. There was a tone of arrogant contempt in their reference to the uncircumcised men, with whom Peter had sat down to eat.

Our Apostles met their charges by a careful narration of the facts. Had he been invested with the absolute authority, with which the apostate Church has credited him, he would never have allowed his brethren to call him to account, would never have pleaded his cause at their bar, would never have summoned witnesses to attest his truth. He would have carried the matter with a high hand, and asserted his supreme and unassailable authority. Instead of this he appealed from men and from himself to God. The descent of the Spirit, identical as it was with their own experience, was the Divine vindication of his action. "If God gave unto them the like gift . . . who was I, that I could withstand God?" To Gentiles who believed the sealing of the Spirit had been given, equally as to Jews who believed. Faith, altogether apart from the presence or absence of any rite, had been the sufficient condition of this sealing. Surely, then, neither circumcision availed anything, nor uncircumcision, but faith working by love. Nothing more could be said. "When they heard these things they held their peace and glorified God, saying, Then to the Gentiles also hath God granted repentance unto life."

The question, however, came up in an acuter form at the First Council of the Church, the proceedings of which are recorded in Acts xv. There again Peter told his wonderful story to prove that God, who searches and knows all hearts, had borne witness to the genuineness of Cornelius's faith by communicating the Holy Spirit as to themselves at the first. He at least made no distinction between the Hebrew and the Gentile. It was sufficient that their hearts were alike cleansed by faith. Why burden them with the intolerable yoke of rites and ordinances, "which had indeed a show of wisdom in severity to the body, but were of no value against the indulgence of the flesh"? He gave it, therefore, as his convinced belief that Gentile and Jew alike would be saved by faith only, through the grace of the Lord Jesus, and altogether apart from the presence or absence of any rite.

These were noble words, but neither they nor the decision of the Council availed to settle the strife between the two parties that rent the Church with their contentions. Indeed, the conservative view became so strong that, as Paul tells us in Gal. ii., Peter quailed before it, and even the amiable Barnabas was led away. It fell, then, to Paul, the younger man, to take up and defend the sentiments which the elder Apostle had so boldly enunciated years before. He withstood him to the face because he was to be blamed. Strong measures were employed, because they were needed. If his later relapse had remained unchallenged, Peter's example and influence would have become, not a rock of foundation, but a stone of offence, which would have led to the confusion of the Gospel and the overthrow of weaklings in the faith.

We may be thankful for the unswerving loyalty with which the Apostle of the Gentiles contended throughout his harassed career for a principle which he may have learnt from Peter, and which he expressed in the noble words that he addressed to his erring friend: "Though we are Jews by birth and not Gentile sinners, we know that it is not through obedience to law that a man can be declared free from guilt, but only through faith in Jesus Christ. We have therefore believed in Christ Jesus, for the purpose of being declared free from guilt, through faith on Christ, and not through obedience to Law. I have been crucified with Christ, and it is no longer I that live, but Christ that lives in me.

XXIII

"I WILL GO WITH THEE TO PRISON"

ACTS xii. 1–25.

"How oft do they their silver bowers leave,
To come to succour us that succour want!
How oft do they with golden pinions cleave
The fitting skies, like flying pursuivant,
Against foul friends to aid us militant!"

Spenser.

AGAIN it was the Passover. "Those were the days of unleavened bread." Fourteen years before Peter had been sent with John to prepare the Passover Feast for his Lord, and as the Apostles were gathered around the table he had avowed his willingness to go with his Master even to prison. Here he was nobly fulfilling his vow. At that Passover also he had slept, but it was the sleep of unwatchfulness, of self-confidence, of the weakness of the flesh. He failed to watch even for one hour with Christ. It was the sleep of the sentry at his post! But here again he slept, but it was the sleep of absolute confidence in the grace of Christ, who would yet deliver him, if it were His will; but if not, would enable him to be faithful unto death. Previously he had slept whilst Jesus prayed; now as he slept, not only did the great High Priest pray that his faith might not fail, but many were gathered together in Mary's house, and were praying for him. But he was not to die. On that first Easter morning an Angel of the Lord descended from Heaven and came and rolled away the stone that closed the tomb where Jesus had been ensepulchred, and now again an Angel would open the prison-doors on an Easter morn.

I. "THE KINGS OF THE EARTH SET THEMSELVES."—"About that time Herod the King put forth his hands to afflict certain of the

170

Church." He was known as Herod Agrippa, and his character bore the infamous brand of the Herod-stock. By unscrupulous subservience to the caprices and crimes of Roman Emperors, and a lamb-like guile beneath which he concealed the passions of the forest, he had become possessed of regal power hardly inferior to that of Herod the Great. In order to ingratiate himself with the Jewish leaders he made a great show of zeal for the requirements of the Mosaic ritual. Josephus tells us that he did not allow one day to pass without its appointed sacrifice. But his further steps in the same direction were taken in the blood of Christian martyrs. Hitherto the Sanhedrists had not ventured openly to oppose the progress of the Church, though they gnashed their teeth against it in mortification and rage. They heartily welcomed, therefore, the policy of persecution and extermination which the King proposed. They even winked at his exercise of the prerogative of death, which they had sacredly reserved within their own jurisdiction. Their hatred of Christ was gratified, and Herod's position was apparently strengthened—were not these results well worth the spilling of Christian blood?

James, one of the Master's innermost circle, was the first to suffer. He had been surnamed Boanerges, and had on one occasion called fire from Heaven. May not his vehement passion for righteousness have been the reason why he was summarily executed by Herod's sword? Perhaps he stood in the breach against the tyrant, and declared the fate which must overtake him, if he continued his persecuting policy—a fate which, as this chapter tells us, did actually overtake him. Did he remind Herod Agrippa of the awful death-scene through which his grandfather had passed to his account? The historian does not gratify our curiosity. All we know is that he proved himself able to drink of his Master's cup and be baptized with His baptism, and that in a chariot of fire he ascended to his throne.

Agrippa saw that it pleased the Jews, and he was encouraged to strike again, but harder; and this time to arrest the leader of the hated sect, who more than once had defied the whole strength of the Sanhedrim. Peter was the strongest element in the Christian community. The precautions taken to secure him suggests that the King feared lest his arrest might lead to an attempt at rescue, and also that his advisers and abetters had a lively memory of the two previous occasions on which the prison-doors had been opened for the release of this same man. Like Pharaoh, like Saul, like Ahab, like Haman, like Antiochus Epiphanes, like Herod the Great, like Nero, Herod Agrippa set himself against Jehovah and against His Christ. A body of sixteen soldiers was set to watch and hold the prisoner. Four were on duty for three hours, and were then relieved. Two were in the cell with him, his hands fastened to one on either side. A third stood outside the bolted door, whilst a fourth was posted along the corridor, which led to the great iron gate. The place of confinement was probably the Castle of Antonia, which was situated between the outer and middle wall. "The wicked plotteth against the just, and gnasheth upon him with his teeth; the Lord shall laugh at him, for He seeth that his day is coming." Already Herod's doom was prepared, and the Angel who was to release Peter was ready to smite the tyrant oppressor in the hour of his greatest triumph. When the people were shouting in mad adulation, "It is the voice of a god, and not of a man," immediately the Angel of the Lord smote him, because he gave not God the glory: and he was carried from the theatre to his palace, a dying man. For five long days he lay in excruciating agony, and on the sixth of August expired, unlamented. As Peter said long after, "The Lord knoweth how to deliver the godly out of temptation, and to keep the unrighteous under punishment unto the day of judgment."

II. THE PRAYER OF THE CHURCH.—The situation appeared desperate, so far as human judgment was concerned. If Herod succeeded in his designs against Peter, what could the rank and file look for but wholesale massacre. If the shepherd cannot stand against the lion, what must the sheep expect? But there is always a weapon left to the children of God. With God all things are possible. It is proverbial that prayer moves the arm that moves the world; but would it not be more accurate to say that it reaches the Heart of Him who has all power in Heaven and on earth? Peter was kept in prison "until the days of unleavened bread had passed"; but prayer was made without ceasing of the Church unto God for him. In the Greek, the word rendered *without ceasing* is used to described the Lord's supplications in Gethsemane, when, "being in an agony He prayed the more earnestly." The wrestlings of the Church on behalf of their beloved leader were only too be compared to the strong crying and tears with which the Saviour sought the Father's help in His supreme hour.

It is more than probable that Paul and Barnabas were present during these memorable meetings. They had brought gifts of money for the relief of their Judæan brethren; but these were not so precious as their sympathy and fellowship. To be fellow-helpers in inter- cession, to blend their hearts in the common anguish and their voices in the common intercession, were their most precious contri- butions to the dire necessities of the Mother Church. Paul could not forget the fortnight that he had spent with Peter years before; and Barnabas would remember him as the means of his own knowledge of Jesus. Could he ever forget those earlier scenes, when the memory of Pentecost was fresh, and he had attracted Peter's loving gratitude, as he laid the price of his estate at the Apostle's feet?

Day after day passed, and the seven days of the Feast had expired. On the morrow Herod would bring his prisoner forth to a mock trial and then a cruel death. As yet there had been no answering voice from Heaven. The Passover moon was waning, the new day was climbing up the sky. We are informed that Peter was not missed till it was day, i.e., sunrise, about six o'clock. Clearly then his release must have taken place between three o'clock, when a fresh quarter- nion had come on duty, and six o'clock when they were relieved. Some time must be allowed for the watch and their ward to become drowsy and fall into a sound sleep. Therefore it may have been about five o'clock in the April dawn that the light shone into the darkness of the cell, and the Angel of the Lord stood by His servant's side. Until that moment, within we will say two hours of the fateful hour, the Church had never ceased its agonized pleadings on his behalf of their chief shepherd. Again the Saviour came at the fourth watch of the night. Again He tarried until trembling faith had almost expired. Again He had taught the old lesson that men ought always to pray and not to faint." "Be patient, therefore, brethren, until the coming of the Lord. Behold the husbandman waiteth for the precious fruits of the earth, until it receive the latter as well as the early rain. Be ye also patient; stablish your hearts: for the coming of the Lord is at hand." "He that cometh will come, and will not tarry."

Meanwhile He was answering prayer by the great peace which He breathed into Peter's soul. He was sleeping between two soldiers, bound with two chains, and guards before the door kept the prison. So his Master slept amid the storm that threatened to engulph boat and crew. Peter's words in after days may be taken as revealing the secret of his tranquillity. He was experiencing the blessedness of those who are reproached for the name of Christ. He was permitted to be a partaker of Christ's sufferings. The Spirit of glory and of God was resting upon him. He was suffering according to the will of God, and was happy to commit his soul in well-doing unto his faithful Creator. Perhaps, also, he pillowed his heart on the never-to-be-forgotten words, which the Lord had addressed to him on the shores of the lake: " *When thou art old*, thou shalt stretch forth thine hands and another shall carry thee whither thou wouldest not." But he was not old. His power was yet in its maturity; and death by crucifixion was not in Herod's power. So he rested in the Lord, and waited patiently for Him, and his mind was kept in perfect peace. Was not this a part at least of God's answer to the protracted intercessions of the Church?

Pray on, O Church of the Redeemed! Jehovah is riding on the heavens to thy help! He is in the midst of thee, thou shalt not be moved; God shall help thee at the dawn of the morning; the Lord of hosts is with thee, the God of Jacob is thy refuge. There is a river, the streams whereof shall make thee glad!

III. THE OPENING OF THE IRON GATE.—God's Angels are always near us. They are sent forth to minister to us who sorely need their succour. Their pure breasts heave with sympathy for our sorrows, and expand with gladness in our joys. We have no need to summon the spirits of the departed—even if we had the power to do it, which we have not—so long as we can reckon on the benign and strong assistance of these pure and loving ministers. Except in extreme cases, as here, they do not manifest themselves, but they are with us always. Our Father gives them charge concerning us, that they should keep us in all our ways. One such had for the whole seven days of his imprisonment been watching by Peter's side, waiting for the precise moment fixed for action by the Lord Himself. Not a moment sooner; not a moment later. When it arrived he cast off his enshrouding veil, and instantly a mild and gentle light fell on the sleeping group, awaking none of them. He had to smite Peter on his side, and call him to arise. Naturally enough he arose, hardly aware that the fetters and chains had ceased to hold him. There was no need, however, for feverish haste. When the Lord goes before His servants and acts as their rearward, they go neither by haste nor flight. The Apostle seems to have been dazed, and needed constant reminders of what he should do in tightening his girdle, putting on his sandals, and assuming his warm outer cloak. In answer to the Angel's summons to follow him, he passed through the door of the cell as though in a dream. "He wist not that it was true which was done by the Angel, but thought he saw a vision." The gleaming light from his form led him past the first and second sentries, but they gave no sign of awakening. "A deep sleep from God had fallen upon them." Did he question whether that mighty iron gate would open? Did the suggestion occur to his hazy mind, that after all they might be arrested by that impenetrable and insuperable barrier? Was he overtaken by the dread which befell the women, almost on that day fourteen years before, when they suddenly said to each other: "Who shall roll us away the stone from the door of the sepulchre?" There is no answer to these inquiries. But we know that when they reached this last barrier it silently opened to them of its own accord. It was swung open and closed again by strong and invincible hands. The morning breath was in Peter's face, as in company with his Angel guide he passed through one street; but that was all, and it was enough, for God is sparing of the miraculous. When our own judgment is adequate for our tasks, we are left to use it. When, therefore, they had passed through one street, the Angel left him, "and *when he had considered the thing* he came to the house of Mary, where many were gathered together and were praying." Mary was sister to Barnabas and the mother of John Mark. There had been no sleep in that home that night. Peter's coming martyrdom was on every heart; and perhaps the hope of his deliverance had faded from their thought. They were resigning themselves to what seemed to be the Lord's will, and only asking that he might be strengthened and upheld in his last hours. This may explain their incredulity when Rhoda, the servant-girl, rushed into their midst with the announcement that Peter was standing at the gate. For precaution's sake she had asked who it was that sought for admittance at that unusual hour; and when she heard his voice, with which she was intimately familiar, for he was a constant visitor there, she recognized it instantly, and in her joy actually forgot to admit him, so he continued knocking. This might have awakened attention and imperilled his re-arrest, but there seemed no alternative and he could only trust that the same loving care which had delivered him from his enemies would now introduce him to his friends.

"It is his angel," they said, "and thou art mad." But her confident affirmations and the continued knocking at last prevailed, and they opened the door, to find that it was even as the girl had said. "And when they had opened, they saw him and were amazed." It was like the Resurrection, when the Saviour, on the Easter night, showed the disciples His hands and His feet, and they disbelieved for joy and wondered. Peter did not enter the house. As soon as he was missed by his guards, search would probably be instituted in the homes of his foremost friends. There must be no presumption on his part. He must use his own wit to evade his foes. Therefore, with a few hurried explanations and directions, with loving greetings to James and the brethren, he departed whilst it was yet dark and went to another place.

We are all liable to find ourselves in prison—the prison of circumstances from which we cannot extricate ourselves; of relationships that restrain our liberty; of consequences issuing from past sins, that threaten us with the silence of death. We sit in darkness, and are bound in affliction and iron. But let us cry unto the Lord in our trouble, let us ask Him to save us out of our distresses. Let us confess our sins and turn to Him for help. He will hear our cry out of the lowest dungeon and will draw near unto us in the day when we call, saying, Fear not. He will plead the causes of our soul, and redeem our life. He will send His Angel noiselessly to lose our chains and open the prison-doors. He will redeem our souls from going down into the pit, and our life shall behold the light. "Oh that men would praise the Lord for His goodness and for His wonderful works to the children of men!"

XXIV

"MY DECEASE"

2 PETER i. 12–16.

"For thee this day let Paradise fling wide its portals,
To God who made thee, God who bought,
And God whose grace thy cleansing wrought,
That hell no part in thee should claim,
Go!—in the all-victorious Name."

Bright.

WHEN THE great issue which led to the summoning of the First
Church Council, described in Acts xv., had been arrived at, there
appears to have been a further agreement as to the respective spheres
of influence to be allotted to the leaders of the Church. It was
obvious that "the Gospel of the uncircumcision"—to use the
phrasing of Galatians ii., had been entrusted by the Divine Lord to
the Apostle Paul. "He that wrought in Peter for the Apostleship of
the circumcision, was mighty in me also unto the Gentiles." To
Paul, therefore, was given the vast Roman world towards the West.
To this arrangement a hearty agreement was given by James, the
President of the Church, Peter, and John. They gave the right hands
of fellowship to Paul and Barnabas, that they should go unto the
Gentiles, whilst they gave themselves to the scattered sheep of the
house of Israel that lay Eastwards.

I. PETER'S ITINERANT LABOURS.—In pursuance of this arrangement we find the Apostle of the Gentiles visiting Syria and the sea-
board of Asia Minor, passing thence to Greece and Rome. It was in
his heart to cover the whole Western world with a network of evange-
lization. "Round about to Illyricum he fully preached the Gospel of
Christ," and even contemplated a visit to Spain, the extreme limit
of the empire towards the setting sun.

Peter, on the other hand, if we may make inferences from hints in his epistles, corroborated by the statements of ecclesiastical tradition, concentrated his labours on the vast multitudes of Israelites who were scattered through the Eastern portion of the Empire. It will be remembered that representatives of the "Diaspora," or scattered Jews, are specially mentioned in Acts ii. as forming part of the vast wondering crowd which gathered on the Day of Pentecost. Parthia, Media, Persia, Mesopotamia, Pontus and Cappadocia, Phrygia and Pamphylia, had sent their contingents; and it is more than probable that these very districts were embraced in the wide area which constituted what we may describe as Peter's diocese. Unless tradition is very much mistaken, the last sixteen or seventeen years of his life were occupied by a wide system of evangelistic ministry. Accompanied by his devoted wife, he passed from place to place with such remarkable success that there was a widespread turning to God from idols, to serve the living and true God, and to wait for His Son from Heaven.

Forty years after his death, Pliny, whom Trajan had appointed Governor of part of the region superintended by Peter, described in a State paper the wonderful predominance of Christianity. The temples dedicated to Jupiter and Mars were deserted, the usual sacrifices were unoffered, whilst the entire population frequented the assemblies of "the pestilent Christian heresy." He admits the purity and blamelessness of the Christian ideals and practice, their solemn oaths to abstain from sin, and their freedom from sins of violence. This testimony is confirmed by others, and as we connect their various testimonies, we obtain the vision of a widespread Christian community animated by passionate devotion to Christ and to the spread of His Gospel among their fellows. "It is incredible," writes one of the historians of the period, "with what alacrity these poor people support and defend their cause. They are firmly persuaded that one day they will enjoy eternal life; therefore they despise death with wonderful courage, and offer themselves voluntarily to punishment. They look with contempt on all earthly treasures, and hold everything in common." Such was the harvest, plentiful and rich, that resulted from the labours of Peter and his fellow-workers in these prolific fields.

The contention that he wrought mainly in the Eastern part of the empire is further supported by the inscription of his First Epistle. He addresses the elect, who are sojourners of the Dispersion in Pontus, Galatia, Cappadocia, Asia and Bithynia, and it is interesting to notice that the order of enumeration is that which an author would use who was writing in the East and not in the West. The enumeration begins with the Easternmost province, proceeds Westward, and ends with the most distant in the South.

This vast area, as large as the whole of France, containing 500 cities and towns, was repeatedly traversed by the Apostle, but it is clear that he was something more than an itinerant evangelist. His Epistles supply evidence that he remained long enough in each place to build healthy Churches, appoint elders, and shepherd, according to the Lord's command, both lambs and sheep. The tone of his Epistles is so affectionate and intimate, his acquaintance with the afflictions and sufferings through which they were passing is so sympathetic, his consciousness that the putting off of his body would be a personal grief to them is so unaffected, that we realize as we read that there was a very evident and tender personal relationship which knit him to them, and them to him. The rendering of the Revised Version—though not the marginal note—suggests also that the elect sister, who was in Babylon, was his wife, who took the opportunity of sending a loving salutation to the wives and daughters whom she had come to know and love. The fact also that the epistle is addressed, not to Churches, but to the elect sojourners of the Dispersion, supports the view that Peter exercised a very distinct pastoral office, which could only have originated in a prolonged residence in the main centres of population.

It must not be supposed, however, that he addressed himself only to Jews. He expressly mentions those who had not been a people, but were now the people of God; who had not obtained mercy, but had now obtained it. It has been inferred from his warnings against the luxurious plaiting of the hair, the wearing of gold, and the putting on of apparel, that the new faith had attracted some of the wealthier classes. Perhaps also his desire that, when called upon, believers should be able to give an apology, or defence, of their hope, indicates that some amongst them were of sufficient culture to do so with efficiency. But clearly there was a vast popular movement towards

Christianity which filled the devotees of the old systems of idolatry with dismay.

There are references to Peter in the First Epistle to Corinth which suggest that he had visited that important city, through which the commerce poured between Rome and Babylon, on account of its central position between the two hemispheres. "I am of Paul, and I of Apollos, and I of *Cephas*"; also, "Have we no right to lead about a sister, a wife, even as *Cephas*?" These may simply refer to the strong conservative party in the early Church which ranged itself under the powerful ægis of his name, as contrasted with the more advanced and liberal school of thought led by Paul. But it is not unreasonable to accept these references in their most literal sense, and to believe that, even after the unfortunate incident at Antioch, Peter, in Corinth, and perhaps elsewhere, personally co-operated with and supported that noble Gospel-pioneer, whom in his Second Epistle he designates as his "beloved brother" Paul.

II. HIS FINAL RESIDENCE IN BABYLON.—In its closing sentence, Peter dates his First Epistle from Babylon, and there is no valid reason for doubting that towards the end of his life, when the increasing infirmities of age placed a necessary restraint on his labours, he made his home in that ancient and historic city, which was densely peopled by Jews.

When Nebuchadnezzar captured Jerusalem on the first occasion he transported to Babylon "the chief men and all the men of might, and all that were strong and apt for war"; and, a few years afterwards, when Zedekiah had revolted, after burning the house of God and breaking down the wall, the great King carried away to Babylon all who had escaped the sword. There was therefore a very large Jewish population in the province of Babylonia, and they were treated as free colonists, with an opportunity of thriving and enriching themselves and the nation, which they were not slow to embrace. The bands that followed Ezra and Nehemiah to their desolated city and denuded lands were a comparatively small percentage of the whole number that had been removed. The rich, the learned, and the high-born seem to have chosen to remain in the beautiful land of Babylon, with its mighty rivers, its luxuriant vegetation, its delicious climate. "The flower of the nation had been carried into exile, and it was the flower of the nation which chose to remain in the land to which they had been deported."

It has been computed that the number of Israelites in Babylon at the time of which we are writing could not have been less than two millions. In his *History of the Jews*, Dean Milman states that the Babylonian settlement was so numerous and flourishing, that Philo more than once intimated the possibility of their marching in such force to the assistance of their brethren in Palestine as to make the fate of war with Rome very doubtful.

These Babylonian Jews were extremely loyal to the great traditions of the past. They have been described as Hebrews of the Hebrews. They forwarded lavish contributions annually to the maintenance of the Temple services, and in religious matters obeyed the mandates of the Sanhedrim. Despite the distance and the difficulties of travel they brought their children to worship in the sacred shrine. It was toward Jerusalem that they turned when they prayed. They might not hang their harps upon the willows of Babylon, but their right hand must lose its cunning before they could forget the city of their fathers. The atmosphere, therefore, which they created for themselves was so Jewish that it became a proverb— "Whoever dwells in Babylon is as though he dwelt in the land of Israel."

We may, therefore, believe that the brave craft which had weathered so many storms found in this great and beautiful city a haven of comparative calm. It was there, also, that the chief pastor of the scattered flock indited the First Epistle, which was distributed through Silvanus, or Silas; and the Second, which may be regarded as his final testimony to the truth of the Gospel, for which he was prepared to die, even as the Lord had foretold. His mention of Silas is most interesting, for we know that he had been the close companion and associate of the Apostle Paul. It is a fair inference that he had been sent by his great leader with a message of love and courage to Peter, amid the growing weakness of age; and that he brought with him a collection of all the epistles in which the Apostle of the Gentiles had enshrined his profound thoughts on the excellency of the knowledge of Christ Jesus his Lord. It is evident from the closing verses of his Second Epistle that Peter read them all, and had found some things hard to be understood; but he loved his friend and brother with chivalrous affection, and acknowledged thankfully "the wisdom which had been given him."

It was in Babylon also that he collaborated the second Gospel with Mark, "my son." The Fathers of the Church, including Tertullian, Clement and Irenæus, agree that in an important sense Mark was the "interpreter" of Peter, and we cannot refuse "the widely spread, consistent, and unbroken conviction of the earlier centuries of Church history." In addition to which there are many characteristics in the Gospel itself which harmonize with this tradition. Keen observers have noticed and specialized a multitude of graphic touches which betray the observation of an eyewitness and participator in the wondrous events of the Saviour's ministry. The pillow in the boat, the green grass of the Five Thousand Feast, the colt tied outside the house, the taking of little children *in His arms*, the mother-tongue of Talitha-cumi, that the face of Peter was towards the fire-light when he was detected, and that the Resurrection message included *and Peter*—have been quoted as evidences that behind Mark's vivid pen there was the recollection of one who had been an eyewitness of the Master's majesty and beauty. It must have been beautiful indeed to have seen Peter's face shining with the light of loving memory as, with Mark at his feet, he recounted again the scenes which had revolutionized his life, and which were the dawn of a fellowship that, maturing through the years, was soon to be renewed in the perfect day.

III. THE CLOSING SCENE.—Much controversy has centred around the question whether the "Babylon" of Peter's Epistle is a figurative name for Rome. It has not been absolutely settled, but from what we have learnt in previous pages of the vast Jewish population of Babylon, and of many incidental confirmatory evidences, there seems no reason for refusing to admit that the Apostle referred to the literal city on the banks of the Euphrates. We know that his chief work was among Jews, that there was a large colony of Jews in Mesopotamia, that the five districts addressed in his Epistle are all Eastern ones, and that their order suggests Babylon as the point of view from which the writer regarded them. All of these lead to the one conclusion. But when that is granted, there remain strong grounds for the belief that the decease, or exodus, of the venerable Apostle took place at Rome.

Dean Alford quotes the following sentence from one of the Early Fathers, Lactantius: "Execrable and noxious tyrant as he was, Nero determined to destroy the heavenly Church and to abolish righteousness; and becoming the persecutor of God's servants, he crucified Peter and slew Paul." This at least is perfectly consistent with the Lord's prediction, that when he was old he would be carried whither he would not, and that his hands should be outstretched in death—a remarkable expression which signified the kind of death by which he would be called upon to glorify God.

After reducing Rome to ashes by the conflagration which his wanton cruelty had kindled, Nero cringed before the passionate resentment of his subjects, and in his endeavour to divert it from himself, lighted on the expedient of imputing the hideous crime to the Christians, whose purity was a perpetual rebuke to his outrageous crimes. The scenes of blood which ensued are too horrible to narrate; but in his search for victims he scoured the empire, striking first and hardest the most illustrious and well-known Christian leaders. Amongst these Paul was certainly one, and Peter was almost certainly another. It is supposed that the warrant for his arrest was given at the commencement of the Neronian persecution, A.D. 64; but the journey from Babylon was long, and it might well have fallen to the following year before he reached Rome. A few years after Ignatius, the aged Bishop of Antioch, was brought in a similar manner. He complained that the soldiers who were commissioned to conduct him to Rome were like ten leopards, and that he was fighting with wild beasts by land and sea, by night and day. It may be that Peter and his wife were subjected to similar experiences.

What befell them in Rome is not chronicled by inspiration. Dionysius, Bishop of Corinth in the second century, states that Peter and Paul suffered martyrdom at the same time; and Jerome, in the fourth century, attests that he was crucified and crowned with martyrdom, his head being turned earthwards and his feet in the air, because he held that he was unworthy to be crucified as his Lord was. Apparently this was not an uncommon practice on the part of the Roman soldiery. Eusebius testifies that several martyrs suffered that cruel form of death. Such was the manner in which he put off his tabernacle. Such was the decease which he accomplished at Rome. By such an exodus—for that is the Greek word—he passed out from this world to the bosom of the Redeemer, whom he had so ardently loved. "Lord," he said on one occasion, "why cannot I follow Thee now?" and the Master answered in effect: "Not now, nor here. Thou hast much to learn and do ere thy warfare is accomplished or thy course fulfilled, but *thou shalt follow Me afterwards.*" That word was now fulfilled, and may we not realize the tender sympathy and ministration of the Prince of sufferers to His suffering friend? His own crucifixion, the marks of which were printed on His hands and side, must have made Him specially eager to mitigate the sufferings of that hour, so far as possible. Certainly He awaited His servant on the other side to give him an abundant and triumphant entrance into the Kingdom and glory of the Father.

A legend has obtained wide currency that, acting on the persuasion of his friends, Peter eluded his gaolers, escaped the prison, and was hastening along the Appian Way, with his back to the city, when Jesus met him. Instantly recognizing Him, he asked, "Lord, whither goest Thou?"

"I go again to be crucified," was the reply.

"Lord, wast Thou not crucified once for all?"

"Yes, but I saw thy flight from death, and I go to be crucified in thy stead."

"Lord, I will return to obey Thy command."

"Fear not, for I am with thee."

The Apostle immediately retraced his steps, returned to the prison, and gave himself up to his gaolers. It is obvious that the legend is not inconsistent with the quick alternations of impulse and devotion, of which we have had many illustrations. All the Evangelists agree in describing the strong oscillations of Peter's character. He said, "Depart from me, for I am a sinful man"; and "forthwith he left all to follow Christ." He said, "Thou shalt never wash my feet," and directly afterwards, "Lord, not my feet only, but also my hands and my head." He said, "Not so, Lord," but within a few hours, "Can any forbid water that these should be baptized!" The legend is therefore in precise conformity to his character; but it is difficult to believe that his impulsiveness had not been finally mastered by the dominant indwelling of the Spirit. And yet, and yet, we have had such repeated experiences of our weakness and failure, that we dare not say that he was altogether perfected. We know that it is in us to deny our Lord, for fear of a servant-girl, when we are young; and to shrink from suffering and martyrdom when we are old. But the Love that loved us when we were dead in trespasses and sins fails not!

There is another ancient legend, which, like the other, is probably mythical; but it embalms a tenderness which is characteristic of those blessed first days. It is thus recorded by Clement of Alexandria—"They say that when Peter beheld his wife led out to death, he rejoiced at her calling of her Lord and her conveyance to her heavenly home; and he cried out, encouragingly and comfortingly, addressing her by name, 'Oh, remember thou the Lord!' Such was the marriage of that blessed pair, and their perfect agreement in those things that were dearest to them."

In his two Pentecostal sermons, and in both his epistles, Peter is revealed as an earnest student of prophecy. It has been said of him that in no character in Holy Scripture can we more plainly trace the way in which the meaning of prophecy gradually dawned upon the understanding. He was ever growing in knowledge as well as grace. Now he quotes Joel, then he understands the rejection of the Stone, presently he will refer to the times of restitution whereof God spoke by the mouth of His holy prophets, which have been since the world began. In the household of Cornelius he insists that to Jesus give all the prophets witness. In his latest Epistle he stirs up our minds that we may remember the words which were spoken before by the holy prophets. He realized that much of their predictions had been fulfilled, in so far as they had testified of the sufferings of Christ, and he knew that his ministry had been in strict accord with them, as he preached the Gospel in the power of the Holy Spirit sent forth from Heaven. But when the full radiancy of that glory broke upon his spirit, and the day-star which had long shone in his heart was extinguished in the full-orbed splendour of God's Presence-Chamber, and as he remembered his former experience on the Mount of Transfiguration, we can imagine him saying again, "Lord, it is good for me to be here." There was no need to build a slight and evanescent tabernacle, for he was in the Father's house of many mansions; and there was no fear of the vision fading, or of the faces of the blessed vanishing. The long night of fishing was over, Jesus had come down to the water's edge to welcome him. He had come forth, girded to serve him. The fire of His Love greeted his spirit with its genial glow. His wounds were healed with the leaves of the tree of life; his weariness was forgotten as the Lord kissed his welcome. Then dear and familiar forms began to gather around him, radiant in the love-light that streamed from the Master's presence; and none of them asked Who art thou? or what place is this? For they knew that it was the Lord, and that they were in the Home which He had promised to prepare.

XXV

LIFE'S AFTERGLOW

2 Peter i. 15.

*"In every nobler mood
We feel the orient of their spirit glow,—
Part of our life's unalterable good,
Of all our saintlier aspiration."*

Lowell.

IN HIS EPISTLES the Apostle stored the thoughts which he was especially anxious should be associated with his memory, and we must needs linger a little longer to consider them; and they may be thus enumerated:

I. COMFORT AMID TRIAL.—The Lord had specially commissioned him to strengthen his brethren, and indeed they were passing through experiences that specially called for comfort and strength. They were reproached for the Name of Christ. They were called upon to suffer as Christians. Their enemies spoke against them as evil-doers, and falsely maligned their manner of life. The trials to their faith, patience, and constancy were "fiery." They resembled the ordeal of scorching flame. In fact, they were called to be partakers of the sufferings of Christ, as though their path lay, as His had done, through Gethsemane and conducted to Calvary. Arraignments before arrogant and pagan judges, the loss of property, the infliction of torture, the scattering of families, cruel scourgings, prolonged imprisonment, death in the arena or by fire—these were their experiences. It has been pointed out that Peter uses the Greek equivalent for the word employed by Tacitus regarding Christians, they were punished as "evil-doers."

In these circumstances, what could be more exhilarating than the Apostle's repeated reminder of the example and constancy of the

Saviour, who had suffered for them, leaving them an example that they should follow in His steps? It was not a strange thing that had happened to them. Christ had once suffered as they were suffering, and they had every reason to be proud of their association with Him in His supreme and unapproachable death. "Rejoice," he said, "inasmuch as ye are partakers of Christ's sufferings." In this he revealed the secret of his own soul. Before his eyes the martyr's death was always present, as his Lord had told him; and he passed on to others the source of his own steadfastness and courage, that Christ who had suffered for him would be near to strengthen and uphold him as he trod the burning embers with his bare feet.

II. The Sacrificial Nature of the Saviour's Death.—That was no ordinary death before which the sun veiled his face and the rocks rent in sympathy. It was the death of the Redeemer. It was a sacrifice, as of a Lamb without blemish or spot. The Son of God had borne the sins of men in His own body on the tree. He had died, the just for the unjust, to bring them to God. The blood shed on the Cross was "precious" blood. Its sprinkling on the conscience brought peace, and severed the soul from its vain conversation received by tradition from the past. The Apostle had been brought to understand that the scene he witnessed, amid the gloom which nearly hid the Cross, was in pursuance of a purpose that was pre-ordained before the foundation of the world. The element of sacrifice had always been present in the nature of God; and it was due to this that the Almighty was warranted in creating beings that could sin. But thence arose the demand that His children should be holy in all manner of life, whilst the crime of neglecting the love, which counted no cost too great, if only it might achieve salvation, was proportionately enhanced. If judgment began with the house of God, what would be the end of those who obeyed not the Gospel of such love, of such infinite value, of such unestimable price?

III. The Certainty of Future Glory.—Those whom Peter addressed were reminded that they had been begotten unto a living hope by the resurrection of Jesus Christ from the dead. For them an inheritance had been purchased and was awaiting them, which was incorruptible, undefiled, and amaranthine. For them a salvation was ready to be revealed, which would cause them to forget their heaviness through manifold trials. Great Grace was to be brought unto them at the glorious unveiling of Jesus Christ. They had been partakers of Christ's sufferings, but His Glory would certainly be revealed, and then they would be glad with exceeding joy, and would receive a crown of glory that could not fade away. They had been called to glory, and God would not belie the hopes He had inspired. On the contrary, He would minister to them an abundant, i.e., a choral and triumphant, entrance into the Kingdom of their Lord and Saviour. The day would dawn after the night of storm. The day-star of the eternal morning would arise and usher in the Day. Though the heavens and the earth should be dissolved and the elements melt with fervent heat, they might confidently reckon on the new heavens and the new earth, "wherein dwelleth righteousness." Such were his anticipations. If Paul may be termed the Apostle of Faith, and John the Apostle of Love, surely Peter is rightly styled *the Apostle of Hope*.

IV. THE URGENCY FOR A HOLY LIFE.—His converts were elect through sanctification of the Spirit unto obedience. They could not fashion their lives according to their former lusts, committed in comparative ignorance. He who had called them was holy, and they must be holy also. They were called to be a chosen generation, a royal priesthood, a holy nation, a people for Christ's own possession; and they must show forth the praises of Him who had called them out of darkness into His marvellous light. By their good works they were to compel the Gentiles to glorify God. The time past had been more than sufficient to have walked in lusts, revellings, and abominable idolatries, and now they must reckon that, like Noah, they had crossed the waters of the deluge of death into the world of resurrection and life.

Our space does not permit of our dilating on all the exhortations to holiness which are found in these Epistles, nor to indicate the qualities of Christian character on which the Apostle insists; but we may specify the one grace of Humility on which he lays special and repeated stress. "Be ye clothed with humility; for God resisteth the proud, and giveth grace unto the humble." How different are these injunctions from the old proud, boastful, and imperious spirit, which in his earlier life had so often betrayed him! He was no longer a lord over God's heritage, but "an example to the flock."

In this connection, also, we should specially study those exquisite passages in 1 Peter ii. and 2 Peter i. The one leading us from the foundation of the Christian character in the living stone to the ministry of the believer in the inner Temple, offering up spiritual sacrifices; and the other enumerating the graces of a holy life, as if they were a choir of blending voices, faith at the extreme beginning and love at the extreme end. Thus the soul of the believer may actually become a partaker of the Divine nature, and escape the corruption that is in the world through lust. Thus also shall we be neither barren nor unfruitful in the knowledge of Jesus Christ our Lord. What a conception is here of the gallant ship having battled its way through storm and danger, coming into harbour with flags flying at the mast-head and greeted by welcoming crowds!

V. The Nature of Death.—He thought and spoke of it as the putting off of the tent or tabernacle, which symbolized the pilgrim-character of his earthly life, that he might enter the house not made with hands, his permanent dwelling-place, eternal in the heavens. He said that it was a decease, or exodus. For him death was not a condition, but a passage. It was no Bridge of Sighs from a Palace to a Dungeon, but one of Smiles and Jubilation from a cell to the blaze of the Eternal Day. It was the crossing of the bar that lay between the limitations of the harbour and the broad ocean expanse.

He humbly hoped that he and those whom he addressed might have an abundant entrance ministered unto them into Christ's eternal Kingdom and glory. But beyond this he counted on the inheritance that was reserved in Heaven for him, and that he would be permitted to partake of the Glory to be revealed. But all was summed up in the vision of that dear face, which he hoped to see as soon as he had crossed over. Jesus had been the day-star of his heart, and Jesus would be the light of all his future, in the City which needs neither sun nor moon, because the Lamb is the light thereof.